W9-ACL-615

# i ♥ my in-laws

# i ♥ my in-laws

An Owl Book • Henry Holt and Company • New York

**falling in love with his family,**

**one passive-aggressive,**

**over-indulgent, grandkid-craving,**

**streisand-loving, bible-thumping**

**in-law at a time**

**DINA KOUTAS POCH**

Owl Books
Henry Holt and Company, LLC
*Publishers since 1866*
175 Fifth Avenue
New York, New York 10010
www.henryholt.com



Distributed in Canada by H. B. Fenn and Company Ltd.

Library of Congress Cataloging-in-Publication Data are available.

ISBN-13: 978-0-8050-8279-1
ISBN-10: 0-8050-8279-4

Henry Holt books are available for special promotions and premiums.
For details contact: Director, Special Markets.

First Edition 2007

Designed by Meryl Sussman Levavi

Art on pages 17, 37, 71, 91, 129, 203 by David Cole Wheeler

Printed in the United States of America

10 9 8 7 6 5 4 3 2 1

To David, my spark

# contents

# i ♥ my in-laws

# introduction

Yours is the story of true love. You met at eHarmony.com. You both like pugs. Your second date was a private tour of the planetarium. Now you share a cell phone plan, shop for organic bread at Whole Foods, and faithfully watch *America's Next Top Model* together. Happily, you've tossed away your highlighted copy of *He's Just Not That Into You,* because now you've met someone who is totally into you.

Congratulations on finding your soul mate—an impressive task in a world of six billion men and women. He understands your ritual of trying on *at least* three shirts before you leave the house. And you overlook his ponytail, even though you hint that 1995 called and wants its hairstyle back. The rose-tinted glasses are firmly affixed, because you're head-over-heels in love.

And then, the unbelievable happens. He arranges for a romantic dinner. He fills your home with roses, and on bended knee, he pops *the* question:

"Do you want to meet my family?"

You sweat. You panic. You rub your clammy palms along your pants and nearly vomit into the foie gras terrine. Then you smile: "Of course, I'd love to meet your family. *When?*" . . . because I need enough time to lose ten pounds, retouch my highlights, get a pedicure, and study up on twelfth-century maritime trade practices, not to mention the early Picasso charcoals.

A brief look at history will tell us that Adam and Eve were the luckiest couple in the world. Yes, they were tempted by a serpent, banished from paradise, and parented sons who murdered each other. But they did not have in-laws. You will.

Sure, you seek guidance from:

- Esteban, a.k.a. magic hands, *your hairstylist,* whose boyfriend's parents don't know he exists.
- Maya, *your coworker,* who hasn't even had a boyfriend in five years and has no idea what you're yammering on about.
- Rick, *the self-help radio host,* who advises to look inside yourself for answers.

But do these people really know what to wear, what gifts to buy, and what to do when vacationing with your entire in-law family next week? Because when you're suspended a hundred feet in the air on a chairlift with your mother-in-law and she asks you about your ten-year plan, you're on your own. And yet, you don't have to be.

In your hands, you are holding the bedrock of practical advice on how to deal with your in-laws. A guidebook. A road map. A beacon of hope and light when, for the fiftieth time, you've told your in-laws what you do at your computer hi-tech company and that your name is Christy, not Crispy.

Finally, desperate daughters-in-law, girlfriends, and fiancées can draw upon a full array of sanity-retention techniques for your first meeting straight through to the day your sweetie's family sells all their worldly possessions as part of spiritual cleansing, and then calls to borrow your coffeemaker.

You can now sidestep pitfalls, blunders, and awkward situations that hundreds of daughters-in-law have stumbled into unaware. Statistics show that—along with money—in-law problems are one of the top causes of divorce. A beaten path lies before you. So, enjoy standing on the shoulders of others who have stood before you. Relish being told stories of in-laws worse than your own! And, savor the next time your sister-in-law challenges you to the game of "who is smarter," because you are.

# 1

# meet the baggage

**You *can* judge a book by its cover.**

EXCERPT FROM THE AUTHOR'S DIARY:

*Tonight I brought flowers, wore a gray wool dress, and offered to help in the kitchen. Yet, somehow I ended up sitting quietly with Nana. "What do you do?" she asked. "I'm a writer," I said. She stiffened. "Do you make money?" I fumbled about my last job, how I had just moved to a new city and was sending out resumés. Finally I blurted: "I'm unemployed." After a moment of slack-jawed silence, my potential grandmother-in-law started panicking, as if I were violently choking on a large piece of falafel. "Hey! She's not working! Why doesn't she have a job? A writer! No job!" Thankfully, they separated us at the dinner table. "Shabbat Shalom, my ass."*

## "Don't Worry, They're Going to Love You!"

Thank your mom for the pep talk. The confidence-boosting lies. The deception. If your own mother had ever told you the truth about this cruel world, then you'd know what to expect from your in-laws.

When you were five years old, she could have slipped this handwritten note into your brown-bag lunch:

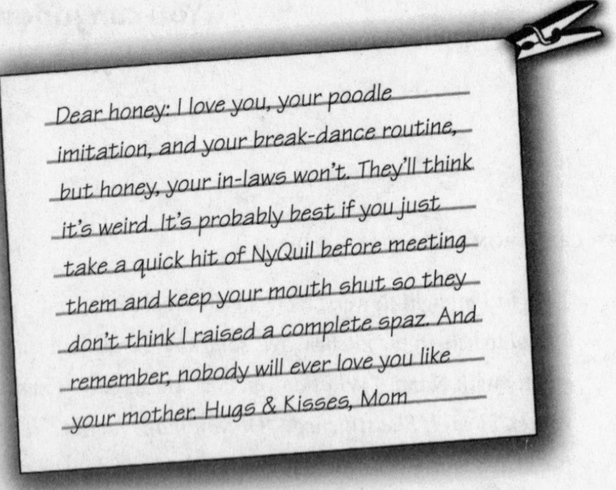

Dear honey: I love you, your poodle imitation, and your break-dance routine, but honey, your in-laws won't. They'll think it's weird. It's probably best if you just take a quick hit of NyQuil before meeting them and keep your mouth shut so they don't think I raised a complete spaz. And remember, nobody will ever love you like your mother. Hugs & Kisses, Mom

She's right. One day your in-laws may appreciate your "letter *Q* prowess" in Scrabble, but no one is going to love you unconditionally like dear old mom. That's why starting on the right foot is imperative, because first impressions last.

You could enjoy decades of blissful marriage, raise wonderful children, make millions, and spend months on space station *Mir*—but your in-laws will still tell everyone that the first time they met you, you were wearing tight little jeans and they could see

THIS MUCH

THIS MUCH

T
H
I
S
M
U
C
H

of your underwear. For the rest of eternity, anytime you screw up, they'll say: "Well, what else did you expect from Little Miss Thongy-Pants?"

By all means, be yourself—your *best* self. Bring your law-abiding, intelligent, fiscally responsible, and fertile self to the meeting with your in-laws. If you're nervous, talk a big game in the mirror before you leave the house. Say something like:

YOU IN THE MIRROR: Dang. You a fine young Betty! What you be trippin' for? Your in-laws best appreciate. Be easy. You're E-class.

But for the love of God, only say that to the mirror, and never in front of his family.

## There's a Second Time for Every Meeting

Perhaps you and yours have been dating for eight years and you can't remember the first meeting with the in-laws (or are trying to forget that they walked in on you two naked in the college dorm room—don't they knock?). You think: do I need to thumb through this chapter? Can't I skip ahead?

There are always firsts, new beginnings, and fresh starts to your in-law relationship. Announcing that you're moving in together, getting married, or having a child will feel like you're meeting them all over again.

So, congratulations on charming your sweetie's ma and pa, and Ma's new "partner," and Pa's third wife, but your work is far from over. Introductions to the in-law family have only just begun. Eventually you will get to share the company of:

- Crazy Uncle Bob, the one who formed his own militia to control immigration along the Canadian border and has the god-given right to bear arms.
- Cousin Pam, the gay conservative Republican. Yes, she votes for people who vote against her. Try espousing that logic at dinner and see where it gets you.
- Baby brother Tom, the one who tie-dyed the family dog for his college application to RISD and has taken a vow of silence until he hears back.
- Linda—you're not even sure who she is, and you can't ask now—she might be somebody's wife, or daughter, or neighbor, or the caterer. But dammit, the two of you are chatting up a storm and she's the only one here who likes you and you don't want to ruin it.

It's overwhelming keeping names straight. Occupations. Religious beliefs. And pet peeves. But you should make the effort, because you're expanding your family tree and will definitely get some great apples in the bag. It's amazing that you now have:

- A vegan chef in-law to help you with your skyrocketing 300 mg/dL cholesterol
- A dermatologist in-law to give you a lifetime supply of retinol skin creams

- A rock star in-law to invite you backstage at the MTV Music Awards

You're adding to your Rolodex, practically doubling your wealth. When you play the in-law lottery sometimes you hit the jackpot. But whether you relish your winnings or cry over your losses, your in-laws and all their glory were responsible for creating the object of your affection—your boyfriend, fiancé, husband, or ex-husband (hey, in-law bonds have been known to withstand divorce).

### In-Law & Order

According to your in-laws, you're guilty until proven innocent. It's like a showdown in the Old West, and they're the sheriff, and you're the bad guy in the black hat with apparently way too much lipstick and eye shadow.

But what crime have you committed? You're dating their son and he's changed. He no longer lives at home. He's no longer a slob. And he's in love. Who are you—*really*? What mind-controlling techniques are you using? For all they know, you might convince their baby boy to move 6,000 miles away with that fancy job of yours and your European flair. *Why the sudden interest in Camembert? Hmm? He's not using our miles to go apartment hunting in Paris!*

Like a good cop–bad cop routine from *Law & Order,* they'll get to the bottom of your nefarious plot.

FATHER-IN-LAW: How did you and our son meet?

YOU: We met at a dinner party.

FATHER-IN-LAW: That sounds nice.

YOU: Yeah, it was—

MOTHER-IN-LAW: You know what else is nice? *Living a lie!*

(A bright light is pointed into your eyes)

FATHER-IN-LAW: Honey, we just want the facts.

(He throws a file on the table. You start sweating.)

FATHER-IN-LAW: We know about the company called L'Oréal and your little interview.

YOU: I don't know what you're talking about.

MOTHER-IN-LAW: Stop playing games with us!

(She throws a Dunkin' Donuts coffee cup against the wall. It's Styrofoam, so it doesn't have the effect she was going for.)

MOTHER-IN-LAW: What are your intentions with our son? Are you moving him to France?!

If you survive the interrogation, you'll be put on the stand, where strategy becomes even more essential. Dodging harsh cross-examination is tricky, but not if you align yourself with the jury. You know who the jury is—the divorced parent who wants back "in" with their son, the awestruck younger sibling, or the grandparent who just enjoys your spunk. Scramble to sit next to them. Pepper them with questions. Flatter them like there's no tomorrow. These people determine your fate: community service vs. death. Girl, you want to live.

Remember, when meeting your in-laws, your partner will lie to you. Maybe it's unintentional, but he doesn't understand the How, When, Where, and What of daughter-in-law life—how you look, when you meet, where you meet, and what you say. He only sees the Who, and he thinks she's terrific.

That's sweet, but utterly useless. When he says, "Don't worry, they're going to love you," lock yourself in a closet and grab this book. Here's what to really expect when they're expecting you.

### Your Partner Says:

**"Don't worry about what you wear. You look amazing in everything!"**

Actually, you don't. So, ease up on the belly T's. Toss aside the flimsy miniskirt (a weak breeze could rip that off!). Now is not the time to show off your rack, your hard earned six-pack, or your "I Love Bobby" tattoo.

It's a job interview, and you want to secure employment as a beloved daughter-in-law. What you wear directly affects your chances. Clean lines and simple tones work wonders. Corduroy pants and a nice turtleneck never hurt anyone. Jaclyn Smith makes a lovely collection for Kmart.

You want to express your spirit and yourself, fine, just do so with restraint. If you normally dress as the missing member of Cirque du Soleil, choose only one color to work with your head wrap and tights. If you have never, ever shaved your legs, this isn't the time to stick those puppies in nude panty hose. Can you say Chia calves?

Work within your comfort zone. Check with someone whose style you respect—your best friend, a European aunt, or your savvy coworker. Likely, she's been dreaming of this makeover since your unfortunate episode with the neon "Orlando, Florida!" tank top and bike shorts.

However, be prepared to defend your Day-Glo hair while standing on their front porch waiting to be let inside. If there are certain personal style choices you're not willing to give up or hide (like that nose ring smack in the middle of your face), you can hope that your in-laws will respect your fashion sense, but you shouldn't be so naive as to think they won't notice. As a general rule, if your clothing, jewelry, tattoos, or gold tooth would give *your* parents pause, don't bust them out on the in-laws right away.

It only takes a nanosecond to make a judgment. The last thing you'd want from your in-laws is for them to air-kiss you good-bye, close the front door, and start taking bets on when you're going to break up.

> "I wanted to dress up and replace my 'vintage' Converse all-stars with a cool pair of heels. But they were so high, I couldn't walk. I was something out of a Jim Carrey movie when I tripped on a carpeted stair in the restaurant and fell into a plant. I looked so drunk. I shouldn't have strayed too far from the footwear I use 364 days of the year. Lesson learned."
>
> AMBER, DAYTONA

**YOUR PARTNER SAYS:**

**"Any time is fine to meet my family. Does it matter?"**

Yes! Timing is critical. There is a right time and a wrong time for introductions. Think twice when Mercury is in retrograde, a black cat crosses your path, or when your boyfriend is announcing to his parents that he is dropping out of medical school to become an actor.

And not just the right time, but *on* time. The early bird gets the worm. The late bird starves to death alone. So please be punctual. When your car is towed right before you're supposed to meet your in-laws at the airport, there are no excuses. No matter the injustices of routine parking violations, your in-laws will believe that you parked beside a fire hydrant in front of a hospital. Now you don't have a car. Now you're late. Now you're not good enough for their son.

It doesn't matter how you get to the United Airlines terminal by 10 PM, just get there. Borrow a car. Hire a car service. Carjack one from an old lady. The choice is yours. One thing is simple: you get zero points for being late and tremendous praise for being committed, punctual, and inventive.

Meeting in-laws is delicate business. There are dates that are good for you, and there are dates that work for your in-law family. Ideally, find one that satisfies you both, but if someone has to compromise, it should be you. You can rise early at 8 AM on a Sunday if it means catching Grandpa Carl before his prostate treatment.

### Game-Time Decision

You just got fired from your job. It's hours before your in-law rendezvous and you're still clutching your desktop stapler. This is not a good day to meet the in-laws. Call your partner and reschedule because one apple martini into the meal, you'll be screaming about your former boss and his sexcapades with Pam, the office intern. No one wants to hear that. No one.

It's also imperative to be welcomed into your in-law family on a happy note. If your man is embroiled in a family feud, his drama will overshadow you, even if you brought a cheesecake. Let your sweetie iron things out before bringing you into the fold. Do you want to be present when he confesses that he lost the family fortune on a racehorse named Limpy? Even though the odds were in Limpy's favor?

Timing is the secret to many happy relationships:

- A Krispy Kreme three seconds out of the oven
- The BeeGees and the 1970s
- Big Bird and Snuffleupagus

- Harry and Sally and when they met
- Pregnancy and the rhythm method

Your in-laws are no exception.

> "The first time I met my in-law family, my younger sister-in-law was debuting her acting for a local cable commercial. We all sat on the couch with popcorn, excited and supportive. We cheered when she flashed on the TV screen. She and another girl were running through a golden field and then started kissing and making out. This wasn't just a surprise to me. It was a surprise to my in-laws. It was so uncomfortable and quiet. I couldn't shove enough popcorn in my mouth."
>
> Pria, Kansas City

**Your Partner Says:**

**"My family doesn't care where they eat. They're chill."**

How can one person be so wrong? When selecting a place to meet your in-laws, find common ground. Embody Switzerland. Sure, the Swiss can be annoying—boasting about Roger Federer, the superiority of their chocolate, and the brilliant writings of Hermann Hesse—but they do have bragging rights for their international political neutrality.

Unfortunately for you, 80 percent of the time your in-laws will insist that you meet on their turf, and over a meal. So, Ms. Manners, are you paying attention? Try to be the nicest dinner guest they ever had, even if you have to spit fishbones into your napkin and kick the dog to stop him from licking your feet under the table. You will be rewarded with homemade pie and whispers of "My, what good table manners Lauren has. I asked for salt and she passed the pepper, too. That girl was raised right!"

Some in-law families won't welcome you into their home until after they've checked you out on neutral ground. Not just any girl gets to sit on those plastic-covered sofas in their parlor! In this case, don't let your in-laws convince you to meet at Hard Rock Cafe, California Pizza Kitchen, or Red Lobster. Loud, packed theme restaurants are places for screaming families and bloated tourists, not first introductions to the fam—no matter how good the Caesar salad is. This isn't a round of golf with Tiger Woods—you don't want to start with a handicap.

How to move your meeting to neutral territory?

**To Get Them out of Their House:**

- Who has time to slave away in the kitchen these days? Not your in-laws. Even if they're gourmet chefs, everyone deserves to be waited on. You have a perfect place in mind that's low-key and in the neighborhood. (Since you're picking the place, you should also spring for the bill. It's only fair.)

**To Change the Restaurant:**

- Mention that you want to take your time with your in-laws, and these types of restaurants rush patrons in search of the next check.
- Did you see that thing? In the paper? About that place with the roaches? You think it was that place.

Of course, situations come where you won't be able to circumvent their turf, such as holiday dinners, birthday parties, and family reunion BBQs. If you can't bring your in-laws to Switzerland, bring Switzerland to your in-laws.

Bear a gift. Something small and thoughtful. Use the chart to help select the right present—a.k.a. the greatest olive branch ever!—for the day your in-laws open their front door.

Double-check with your partner about what is appropriate. A dessert loaded with peanuts is an insult to a family with nut allergies—it's the equivalent of handing them the family dog's head on a platter:

> "I baked a delicious pumpkin pie for my in-laws. I expected to be exalted for my culinary achievements; instead, my grandmother-in-law hobbled past the kitchen counter, gagged, spat, and banged her cane, yelling at anyone who would listen how much she hates pumpkin pie. 'Who brought this pie?' Even in her nightgown that night, she continued to interrogate and question about the pie-bearer . . . me!"
>
> LYNN, AUSTIN

**YOUR PARTNER SAYS:**

**"Everyone calls him Frank. Everyone."**

It's upon you, and only you, to play the name game early and learn, firsthand, what to call your in-laws. Do they go by titles—Lorenzo the Magnificent? Will they send mixed messages—"Please, call me Frank" but then refer to himself as Mr. Smith? Clear the air immediately. Ask directly: "How should I address you—Sir, Ma'am, Mrs. Culpepper, or Mommy?"

Your sweetie also neglected to mention that his family engages in the sophomoric pastime of assigning nicknames—Spears for Britney, DinaDinaBoBina for Dina, or Sweet-Lips

# Gifts to Break the Ice

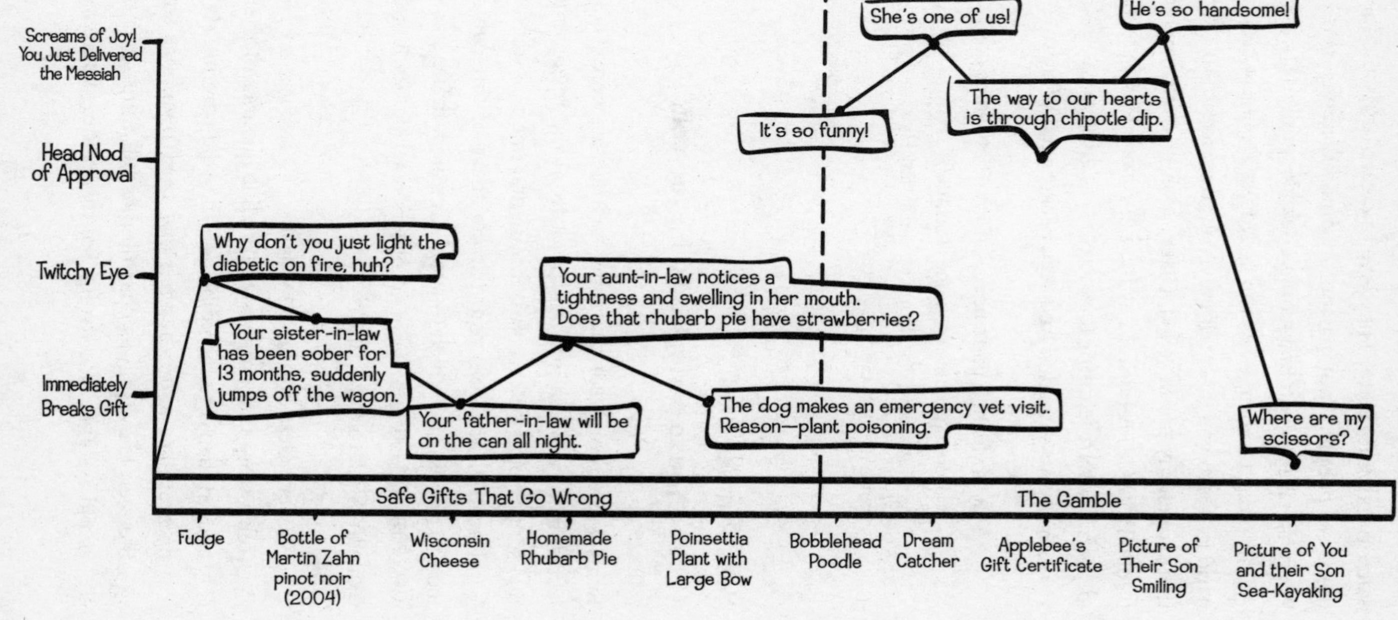

Salmon Cakes for Kate. They love to create labels and then slap them on people. Your partner's Jamaican nanny was "Mary Poppins." Watch out: nicknames stick like gum to sneakers.

In order to change it, refer to yourself often. Create a scenario in which you repeat, loudly, your own name. You say: "And that's when my friend yelled, Claire, look it's your name on the JumboTron! C-L-A-I-R-E! How funny!" Also, pretend you have no idea who they are referring to when they address you as "E-Claire." Look over your shoulder. And then back, again. Who, me?

> "My boyfriend's dad's name is Rick. That seems normal enough, but his name is actually George. His kids call him Rick. His wife calls him Rick, but his name is really George. Okay."
>
> JEN, MINNEAPOLIS

### YOUR PARTNER SAYS:

**"You're perfect. Just be yourself."**

Regis wasn't born *that* charming and neither were you. Preselect dinner conversations and read from the teleprompter. A real script might be creepy, but a mental one will stand you in good stead. Learn from your partner ahead of time which subjects to discuss and which to avoid. Certain families *love* talking about their dead relatives, and others react by bawling uncontrollably. Stick to the script.

1. **Flattery Gets You Everywhere**
   Tell a story that emphasizes the fine qualities of their child and, in turn, the incredible job they did parenting. Parents and families adore hearing that their own is as smart as Stephen Hawking, as charming as Bill Clinton, and as intrepid as Lance Armstrong. For this evening your sweetie is

no mere mortal, he's a demigod. His solution to the graphic design problem at work saved the company hundreds of dollars—maybe billions of dollars! A toast for the hero is in order! Hip-hip hooray!

2. **Just the Highlights from Your Resumé**

   By preselecting conversation, you're prepared to discuss your own positive qualities. But don't let hubris get in the way of having a good time. It's impossible to bore your in-laws with stories about how perfect their child is, but it *is* possible to drone on too long about yourself. So, you're a successful filmmaker who won the Palme d'Or at the Cannes Film Festival and Martin Scorsese is naming his next child after you? Preserve the balance with everyone else's accomplishments. Your sister-in-law sold the fridge in the garage on Craigslist. It's impressive, 'kay? And she wants to talk about it—*all night long*.

3. **Attention All Nitwits!**

   Don't pretend to be an expert. If you know zilch about string theory and you're sharing a table with physicists, don't passionately bully them that string theory hasn't technically been proven (Einstein only alluded to it). You're out of your element. And it's killing them.

If the conversation veers wildly off-script, prepare smaller topics to reel it back. This is an effective tactic for any of the following scenarios:

4. **The Mr. Smarty-Pants-In-Law**

   If an in-law dominates the conversation and acts intellectually superior by discussing Russia's modern reconstruction policy, steer the conversation toward your unparalleled knowledge of knitting. As an example, segue . . . everyone loves a well-made balaclava, including the Russian oil barons. This way you're contributing to the conversation and proving that you were listening to their lecture all along.

5. **A Man and His Past-In-Law**

   By now, you know most of your in-law family skeletons. But there's an elephant in the room the size of a cruise ship. Uncle Nicky recognizes his former parole officer in the restaurant. Awkward! Now is the time to focus conversation on your in-laws' recent vacation in Aruba. This way Uncle Nicky gets off the hook. His parole officer isn't stared at. And you are slightly less uncomfortable. Strong work.

6. **Hillary Clinton-In-Law**

   When an in-law starts arguing about a politically charged and highly contested topic such as reparations for slavery, rise above the tension and introduce a less controversial one—the adorable pickle costume your partner wore as a kid every Halloween. Everybody smiles when they think about a pickle.

Your in-laws don't want anything less than perfect for their baby. So, ease into their conversation style. Does his family divulge or sit in silence? If you have chatty in-laws and you're too quiet, they'll be suspicious. Too much yammering, and you're uncivilized. Match their style. It's an elaborate dance. They step forward; you step back. Mirror them, and they'll love you, because they love themselves.

> “At a family picnic, I started talking about the time Tyra Banks wore a fat suit for 24 hours. Tyra was shocked to feel so invisible to the world. Hello!”

percent of the world is overlooked when you don't look like Tyra Banks! That's when I realized that my sister-in-law not only loves Tyra, but recently lost 150 lbs. Now I wait for someone else to get the dinner conversations started."

CASEY, LOS ANGELES

**YOUR PARTNER SAYS:**

**"My family is totally bland."**

Lies! Lies! All of them, lies! As soon as he mentions "bland," you can bet that he has descended from a freakish line of wolf people. Or at the very least, swingers. But even if your in-laws are not vulpine sex maniacs, there may still be quirks you can't possibly prepare for.

You open the door and your aunt-in-law has a lazy eye. Is she staring at your hair? The wall behind you? Is she speaking to you? It's hard to tell. Here are a few more things your sweetie dusted under the rug—the same rug that will be promptly pulled out from beneath you.

- **Really bad hair:**
  It's the kind of hair that makes children stare and ask Mommy, "Why?"
- **Horrific body odor:**
  It's so pungent, you think it's you that smells. Maybe your coat?
- **Dandruff:**
  How can your in-law not know? It's a blizzard of scalp all over their head and shoulders.
- **The Joker:**
  This guy gives you a friendly slap on the back to attach a "Kick Me!" sign.

- **An eye patch, a taped nose, and large Band-Aid across the cheek:**

  You don't know what happened and can't concentrate until someone explains it.

- **Mumbling or stuttering:**

  We all know that Winston Churchill stuttered and he was brilliant, but you suspect your in-law is not.

- **Chain smoker:**

  You can barely see your in-law through the thick blanket of smoke that fills the house. And when you do catch a glimpse, he looks like a thousand-year-old sarcophagus with yellow teeth.

- **A high-pitched voice or a low-pitched voice:**

  Either way, you're confused. Have shape-shifters invaded this person's body?

- **Nervous laugh:**

  What's so funny? Did you say something?

- **Nail biting:**

  You know that ten seconds after you're out the door, they're going for the toenails.

"The first time I met my in-laws was at a dinner party at their house. Also in attendance was their great-aunt, Trudy, who considers herself clairvoyant. I noticed her glaring at me. Suddenly, mid-sentence, she stood up and started screaming: 'I know who you are! You're a bad, bad person!' over and over again until my mother-in-law had to ask her to leave. It was a little awkward."

AMBER, SAN FRANCISCO

**YOUR PARTNER SAYS:**

**"You're nothing like my mother."**

Welcome to Oedipus's complex. You're exactly like his mother. In fact, you really like his mother, because she is you and you are she. And you like yourself. There's no shame in that.

You observe the striking similarities, but don't tell your significant other. You don't want him to gouge his eyes out.

As much as you're reeling from this discovery, so is your mother-in-law. Just like you get mad at yourself sometimes, your mother-in-law will frustrate you. She'll finish your sentences. She'll buy the shirt you wanted in the color that wasn't in stock. You can hate her all you want but she already knows that. In fact, she knows that you're reading this right now.

How do you deal with the in-law that is you, just twenty-five years older?

- Observe what your man likes about his mom—her generosity, her nurturing instincts—and silently know that what he's saying about her, he is also saying to you. Of course, this one works both ways, so if he hates Mom's iron grip over the household finances, maybe you should offer to let him balance the checkbook once in a while.
- Be careful not to side with his mom every time they have a fight. Of course, you see her point of view, and that your partner clearly doesn't realize the importance of Tivo-ing *Dancing with the Stars* instead of the Ohio State game. It'll be too transparent if you always agree with your mother-in-law on such matters. Remember, you don't want him to find out that he's dating his mom . . . and then gouge his eyes out.
- She's spent decades molding your partner's dad to her will. Study her technique. Adopt her strategies. Learn how she

replaced his high school letter jacket with a nice peacoat. It's called "tag teaming."

"My mother-in-law always makes a scene in a restaurant. No matter where we eat, our food is sent back to the kitchen for being too cold, too hot, or too salty. If you're paying for something and you want it your way, complaining makes sense! I would totally do the same thing, but since she does it, I don't have to."

JILL, WOODSTOCK

**YOUR PARTNER SAYS:**

**"I've told my parents about us. They know everything."**

They know everything, except that you're gay lovers and not "roommates." You definitely don't want to be the one who outs their daughter, now do you? Okay, secretly it's eating you up, but you can't say anything!

Of course, you'll throw clothes into the second bedroom and pretend for a week that you're not madly, completely head-over-heels in love, but rather are best-friend roommates who share underwear. It may take a while for your sweetie's parents to acknowledge your union. However, in due time, if you seem healthy and happy and perfect for each other, and are inclusive of your in-laws, you may land on the cover of *Lilith* magazine.

"My partner and I had been dating for almost a year, but we had never told her Southern Baptist mother. It wasn't something we were ready to do. We were in love and that was all that mattered. After staying with my mother-in-law for a long weekend, she insisted that we all watch her favorite soap opera. She really made a stink about it. Well . . . the main story that day was about two of her favorite female characters falling in love. Afterward, she smiled and hugged us both. We never had to say anything but she knew and accepted. I almost cried. Three cheers for *As the World Turns*!"

EVA, CHAPEL HILL

However stressful it is for you to be introduced into your in-law family, know that it's just as hard for them. You're worried about your outfit; they're obsessively cleaning the den. You're memorizing the players on their NFL team; they're learning to pronounce your name. It's Cheryl. How hard is that? In the end, they're nervous about you liking them, too. You're dating their baby, brother, nephew, and cousin, and if you don't like them, they're only going to see him once a year when he visits while you're in Vegas with the ladies.

When in doubt about how to behave, channel Ms. Emily Post. She would tell you that meeting your in-laws is not the time to answer your cell phone, run your hand up your boyfriend's pant leg, or discuss the virtues of medical marijuana. Rather, your in-laws enjoy when you ask sincere and informed questions about them.

Treating their baby right and showing interest in the family are the best compliments you could ever pay to them—that and sending a thank-you note. By "showing an interest" we mean learn who you're dealing with. In-laws come in many shapes, colors, and sizes. What have *you* inherited?

# 2

# know thy enemy

**Knowing is half the battle.**

EXCERPT FROM THE AUTHOR'S DIARY:

> *My father-in-law had foot surgery last week. Now I know his true nature. He will "win"! He's healing quicker, eating better, walking faster, and forming less scar tissue than any other patient. He's doing extra leg exercises while others sleep (on the job). He threw away his crutches—who needs them? He's the Michelangelo of bone healing. What kind of father-in-law am I dealing with? In a matter of days, he'll be lifting a car with his bare hands, wearing an ankle brace, while I sit on the couch watching the* E! True Hollywood Story *of Ally Sheedy.*

## Reconnaissance Mission

Know thy enemy. Sizing up your in-laws is key toward leveraging power over them. Not everyone is an open book. You have to dig deep. The next time your in-laws bust out the family photo album, don't let your eyes glaze over and "go to your happy place." Instead, commit scenes and faces to memory. You never know what might unlock a family secret—and secrets are critical to gaining power in your in-law relationship.

All warfare is based on deception. So, don't feel bad about pretending to be a sweet daughter-in-law while analyzing your foe. Because as you read this, the Navy SEAL your in-laws hired to dig up dirt on you is in your apartment thumbing through your mail, smelling your laundry, using your facial toner, and wire-tapping your phone.

## Gathering Ammunition

You're in the attic at your in-laws' house and you find a dusty, pink box marked "Private."

You crack it open by banging it with your flashlight and discover that your mother-in-law nearly married a NASCAR driver. Here's what you should do. Head immediately to Dover International Speedway. Buy your quiet mother-in-law all the Zimas she can drink. Nod knowingly when she tells you she can't taste the alcohol. Is that your sweetie's mom taking her top off and screaming for Dale Earnhardt Jr. to "let her change his oil"? She's putty in your hands.

From the stacks of old journals they mistakenly sent to your house when they were "purging" their material possessions, you learn that your liberal in-laws (the ones who live in a shack thirty miles north of Boulder) once believed in trickle-down economics? Bull's-eye! The absurdity of such a conservative point of view! Then, something shiny catches your eye. There, stuck between the pages of Monday, May 4, 1981, and Friday, May 8, 1981, is a rusty "Go Reagan!" pin. Wow. Throw *that* in their organic soy lattes, the next time they bully you for wearing leather.

*The Art of War* states that to be victorious in battle one must "know thy enemy." Sun Tzu neglected to mention that warriors should also pack dry socks (because nobody likes trench foot), but where he faltered, you will succeed. Learn your in-laws' Achilles' heel to stay one step ahead on the battlefield and avoid ambush.

## War Games

Let the games begin! It's Saturday night and you've just arrived at your in-laws' house after a harrowing 14-hour flight delay. Your skin has not touched fresh water in 36 hours. The taste of airport Pizzeria Uno pepperoni lingers in your mouth. You brush your teeth in the guest bathroom, examining your bloodshot eyes in the mirror, when a knock sounds at the door. It's your mother-in-law. *Maybe she's bringing fresh towels? Or triple-confirming tomorrow's trip to the Howe Caverns?*

### Scenario 1: Taken Hostage

> The bathroom door opens. She's in curlers. It's all a hazy blur before you're kidnapped. Toothbrush in hand, your mother-in-law forces you to examine the subtle differences in the Benjamin Moore Off-White Serenity Paint Collection. Navajo White. Arctic White. Dove White. Almond White. She tells you her plan to remake her bedroom into an ancient Grecian

Villa. White stucco walls. White curtains. White sheets. White Corinthian columns. *Does she notice your disinterested body language? Your caged animal expression?* You wildly gesture to your sweetie in the hallway. He thinks you're having a wonderful time "bonding," waves back, and walks away. You rub your dry toothbrush against your gums. Like a prisoner of war, you make friends with a spider climbing the lampshade, name it Ariella, and whisper to her a story about when you were a little girl.

**Strategy:**

Sun Tzu says: "Seizing the enemy without fighting requires the most skill." Tune out her interior decorating drivel and focus on your escape. Offer to show her a great example of Grecian white in the *American Airlines Magazine* you lifted from the plane, located in the other room with your sweetie. Or slowly build a "human pillow decoy" and slide out of the room on your belly.

### Scenario 2: Cloak and Dagger

You brush your teeth in the guest bathroom, examining your bloodshot eyes in the mirror, when a knock sounds at the door. It's your mother-in-law and she's crying. Immediately, you spit out your toothpaste and hand her a tissue. *What happened? Was she chopping onions? Did Hope Brady from* Days of Our Lives *get brainwashed again?* She informs you that everyone ordered Mexican food for dinner. She wipes her nose and continues: "They *know* how sensitive I am to spicy food. They *know* it gives me gas." Her voice rises. "Can you go downstairs and ask them to order something else? I mean, am I *so* invisible?" Then, she starts howling. Between her rapid breaths, she also mentions that so-and-so didn't call on her birthday twenty-five years ago. You sit down on the fuzzy pink toilet seat cover and elevate your feet. She's only getting started.

**Strategy:**

Sun Tzu says: "Do not enter alliances until acquainted with the designs of neighbors." If you know your mother-in-law will attempt to corner you, lock all doors behind you as you move through the house. If you do get caught, do not enter into an alliance that will alienate you from the rest of the family. She's got designs on you, kiddo—she wants a partner in pasta, an enemy of enchiladas. Tell her they won't listen to you, either.

### Scenario 3: Land Mines

You're brushing your teeth in the guest bathroom. Yes, it's a little creepy in this room, but you don't dwell on it. You spy a magazine, but it's an issue of *Life* from the summer of 1984. *Is that Mary Lou Retton on the cover?* You flip open the toilet seat, admiring its shag cover. Brittle and yellow, the toilet paper crumbles in your hand. *Strange*, you think. That's when you hear it—the frantic knocking on the door. It's your mother-in-law. "Honey? Honey! There's been a mistake. No one uses this bathroom. It was Nana's. Pack your things and use the bathroom downstairs." Suddenly, it makes sense: The crusted Selsun Blue in the shower, the Water Piks, the glass swans beside the sink, the frayed toothbrush, the decaying Maalox bottle. The room is exactly as Nana left it twenty-two years ago, and you're the first one to unwrap her Latvian hand soaps in two decades. But the real question remains: Why are you sleeping on an air mattress while Nana's queen-size bed goes empty?

**Strategy:**

Sun Tzu says: "A leader who moves with confidence anywhere in his environment is on the path to victory." You must not allow strange terrain and unfamiliar environs to throw you off your path. Channel Nana as you pat your mother-in-law on the shoulder and gently steer her from the sanctuary. Begin telling her a story about the Old Country and watch as *her* eyes glaze over. If you can move with confidence in a dead woman's bathroom, having relations with your sweetie on the Aerobed will be a snap.

If your in-laws' secrets are buried deep, hard to reach, or sealed tighter than Fort Knox, use the following quiz to dig below the surface to learn what you're up against.

## ♥ ♥ ♥ ♥ ♥ Sizing Up Your In-Law ♥ ♥ ♥ ♥ ♥

**Q U I Z**

From clothes to decorating taste, to hobbies and majors in college, identify what kind of in-law you have and how much work is ahead of you. Recognize whether your father-in-law would rather be complimented or argued with, and whether your mother-in-law speaks her mind immediately or will wait a year to tell you how she feels, in an e-mail.

---

**1.** Money aside, what would your mother-in-law love to do with her retirement?

a) Decoupage until death's hand rips the glue stick from her fist
b) Drink herself silly
c) Return wolves to their natural habitat
d) Run away on the back of a Harley belonging to a guy named "Bear"

---

**2.** If your father-in-law appeared on TV, what would it be for?

a) A high-speed police chase after stealing an ice-cream truck

b) Answering the question: "He was a Mesopotamian king and epic superhero" correctly with "Who is Gilgamesh?"
c) Arguing in *The Situation Room* with Wolf Blitzer
d) Smiling and waving an "I Love Kelly Ripa" sign at the Macy's Thanksgiving Day Parade

---

**3.** Your mother-in-law thinks that terrorists . . .

a) Are everywhere
b) Are plotting to attack her rural town in Idaho
c) Probably went to art school
d) Have a good point

---

**4.** True or false?

My sister-in-law just sampled all 28 flavors from Baskin-Robbins and didn't buy a scoop.

---

**5.** What is your stepfather-in-law most proud of?

a) Running the V-strike play during the Louisiana State football championship in 1956
b) Serving his country in Vietnam, *boy*
c) Not needing Viagra
d) His home-grown tomatoes

---

**6.** True or false?

My uncle-in-law is shopping for himself in Wal-Mart's women's lingerie department right now.

**7.** What is your mother-in-law's favorite sound?

a) The credit card machine
b) Celine Dion
c) The wrapper peeling off a Snickers bar
d) It must be her Chihuahua yapping because that damn dog never shuts up

---

**8.** Your brother-in-law arrives unannounced on your doorstep. He is . . .

a) Looking for a place to hide from his wife
b) Dropping off a 200-gallon fish tank that he bought you for your engagement
c) Trying to sell you something
d) Breaking into your home

---

**9.** True or false?

Your home-schooled nephew-in-law just asked you to correct his proof on quantum chromodynamics.

---

**10.** The rental car your father-in-law reserved isn't available. What would he do?

a) Punch the #1 Club Gold sign and start shredding the complimentary Hertz maps until security escorts him away
b) Quietly suffer, squeezing his large bags into a Hyundai Accent
c) Convince the staff to upgrade him—*who's driving in style now, baby?*

d) Fake an accent and pretend he doesn't understand the situation

---

**11.** Both your parents-in-law think that your two-year-old child should:

a) Learn Hebrew
b) Get a job
c) Not go to bed if he doesn't *feel* like it
d) Prefer them to the "other grandparents"

---

**12.** True or false?

At any Asian restaurant, my brother-in-law speaks Korean to get free food.

---

**13.** It's 3 PM on a Tuesday. What is your mother-in-law doing?

a) Talking with her sister, again, about Oprah
b) Daydreaming about quitting her job at IBM to plan your wedding
c) Decorating her work desk with more house plants
d) Flooding your in-box with e-mail forwards

---

**14.** What does your father-in-law unequivocally support?

a) The Troops
b) UCONN's Lady Huskies
c) The little guy
d) Strict enforcement at the 12-item or fewer checkout line

**15.** True or false?

Your aunt-in-law is a celebrity judge at the National Harmony A Cappella Competition.

---

**16.** Your mother-in-law would like to talk to you . . .

a) Every day with her morning coffee
b) Once in a blue moon, when she sees a woman that vaguely looks like you
c) Via e-mail, so there's a paper trail of your correspondence
d) Just so long as you don't talk back

---

**17.** How would your stepfather-in-law describe himself?

a) A Sagittarian
b) Polish-American!
c) Successful, because I earned it
d) Hungry

---

**18.** True or false?

My brother-in-law is *probably* losing money right now.

---

**19.** Two trains leave the same station. Train A leaves the station traveling at 40 mph. Train B leaves the station 60 minutes later traveling at 60 mph. When does Train B pass Train A? Your mother in-law would say:

a) Why are they taking the train?
b) I'm going to buy tickets for Train C; it leaves an hour later and my daughter-in-law has *such* trouble with time, so when she shows up late, I'll be prepared!
c) $t - 1$ hr $+ 40t$, 3 hrs

d) Can trains pass each other? That doesn't sound very safe.

---

**20.** True or false?

My father-in-law *would rather* be naked right now.

---

**21.** Your grandmother-in-law annoys you by:

a) Cheating at mahjong
b) Refusing to wear her hearing aid
c) Using her knitting needles as toothpicks
d) Making you sit at the "kids' table"

---

**22.** Your older sister-in-law believes she helped your sweetie pass the Missouri bar exam by:

a) Praying to Jesus every night
b) Letting his law professor touch her boobs
c) Attending law school first
d) Pressuring him to succeed since he was in diapers

---

**23.** What will your mother-in-law wear at your wedding?

a) A brown cotton shirt-dress that covers her knees, arms, and neck
b) A dress that's sexier than your wedding dress, in a size 4
c) A black suit with a black hat for mourning
d) A piece of jewelry that requires a bodyguard

---

**24.** True or false?

The following Rorschach inkblot test made your stepmother-in-law cry:

**25.** True or false?

Your brother-in-law doesn't eat meat he didn't shoot.

---

**26.** Your parents-in-law think the computer is:

a) Something to put flower vases on top of
b) A godsend—there's no other way to order Lands' End underwear
c) A reason to call you at 1 AM for tech support
d) The most wonderful place to find a friendly community of fellow Croatian pornography lovers

---

**27.** Ideally, your mother-in-law would love to remarry . . .

a) Jamie Foxx
b) Her son
c) Any man in uniform
d) Her Latino trainer

---

**28.** How would your sister-in-law finish the following Haiku?

O' Sister-in-law
Will you be sunshine or rain?
_____ _____ _____ _____ _____

a) Haikus schmaikus. Eh.
b) All girlfriends destroy.
c) Hope you last one month.
d) Nice shoes. Can I have?

---

**29.** You call your stepfather-in-law. The phone rings . . .

a) Never: a recorded message tells you the phone is disconnected
b) Once: he's been waiting for your call all day
c) Four times: he's in the woodshop building a large sundial
d) Indefinitely: only sissies gab on the phone

---

**30.** I can annoy my mother-in-law by doing *what*?

a) Limiting the wedding guest list to 200
b) Feeding her dog from the table
c) Feeding her son from the table
d) Not calling her Mom
e) Calling her Mom
f) All of the above

## Summary of Quiz

| | Harmless | Grating | Maddening | Intolerable | |
|---|---|---|---|---|---|
| **Question** | **0** | **1** | **2** | **3** | **Score** |
| 1 | D | C | B | A | ______ |
| 2 | D | B | C | A | ______ |
| 3 | B | C | A | D | ______ |
| 4 | FALSE | | | TRUE | ______ |
| 5 | B | A | D | C | ______ |
| 6 | FALSE | | TRUE | | ______ |
| 7 | A | C | B | D | ______ |
| 8 | B | C | A | D | ______ |
| 9 | FALSE | | TRUE | | ______ |
| 10 | B | C | D | A | ______ |
| 11 | B | A | C | D | ______ |
| 12 | FALSE | TRUE | | | ______ |
| 13 | B | A | C | D | ______ |
| 14 | B | C | A | D | ______ |
| 15 | FALSE | | TRUE | | ______ |
| 16 | C | B | A | D | ______ |
| 17 | B | D | C | A | ______ |
| 18 | FALSE | | | TRUE | ______ |
| 19 | C | A | D | B | ______ |
| 20 | FALSE | | | TRUE | ______ |
| 21 | C | A | D | B | ______ |
| 22 | C | A | B | D | ______ |
| 23 | C | A | D | B | ______ |
| 24 | FALSE | | TRUE | | ______ |
| 25 | FALSE | | | TRUE | ______ |
| 26 | A | B | D | C | ______ |
| 27 | A | C | D | B | ______ |
| 28 | A | C | A | B | ______ |
| 29 | C | D | C | B | ______ |
| 30 | A | B or C | D or E | F | ______ |
| | | | | **Total=** | |

| **Cakewalk** | **Tightrope** | **Dead Man Walking** |
|---|---|---|
| 0 – 20 | 20 – 50 | 50 – 70 |

CAKEWALK

**If you scored less than 20 points:** Place this book alongside your copy of *Ulysses* and *How Proust Can Change Your Life,* to show houseguests how smart you are. Your in-laws are a wee bit quirky, but harmless. You can skim this book and bring only a stress-relief ball and a good exit alibi to the next family barbecue. But be warned—even the most benign of in-laws age. And like fine wine and cheese, they can grow stinky and fermented with time.

TIGHTROPE

**If you scored between 20 and 50 points:** You might want to invest in some Pepcid Antacid, caller ID, and a yoga mat. It's not imperative that you finish this book tonight, but it should be a high priority, missy. As you read this, your in-law is clipping newspaper articles on "How to keep a Clean House" and "Working Mothers Do Finish Last" to send to you. Keep multiple copies of this book handy (in the car, in the gym locker, and the audio version on your iPod)—you never know when in-laws will attack.

DEAD MAN WALKING

**If you scored more than 50 points:** Have you ever seen an empire penguin walking alone on an ice floe? It brings tears to the eyes. No companionship. No food in sight. Nature is a cruel, cruel mistress. And your in-laws are *worse* than anything you find in nature. Your in-laws are deviant. Shifty. Stress makers. This book should become your Bible, your Koran, your Torah. Proceed directly to the next page. Don't stop for a bathroom break, an e-mail check, or that bagel sitting in the toaster. After you memorize each page, tear it out and eat it. You need all the help you can get.

## The Seven Personalities of In-Laws

You took the quiz. You asked yourself the tough, hard-hitting questions. Now, what to do with your mounting insight? The answer: place your in-laws in a box. I know, it seems too simple, too easy. It took decades for people to grapple with the Copernican solar system; likewise, accepting seven categories of in-laws will take some getting used to. But it's time to identify precisely who you're dealing with and get enlightened.

### 1. THE DEAD IN-LAW

**Controls from the grave and still on your guest list**

**College:** The College of Hard Knocks

**Occupation:** Soldering the green wire to the red wire to make radios for RCA

**Voted in high school:** Sainthood

**Hobbies:** Inserting oneself into daily conversation; being immortalized

**Cause of death:** Doesn't matter. It was *too* sudden for everyone.

This in-law manipulates by spreading gloom over life's happiest events. The dead in-law is more intrusive than any live guest. At baby showers, birthday parties, bat mitzvahs, and graduations, this in-law turns on the waterworks from beyond the grave. The scene is the same each time:

> A happy party reveler jumps up. She joyfully grabs the microphone. She's sweaty from dancing. She makes people laugh,

> telling jokes. And then it happens. Dead relative's name is mentioned, and it's like a cloud of black ash blew into the room. People dry their red eyes, hug, and breathe heavily.

Yes, we know! It's very sad that you died, but can we get back to B-52's "Love Shack"? It was bringing the house down. Thanks again, dead in-law, because now the band has to play over people wailing, pounding their chests, and howling your name.

This in-law controls so many parts of your life. You're swimming in heirlooms. You're wearing her mink stole. You're driving his car. But why, dead in-law, do you also control road trips? Your sweetie's family is forever veering three states over to visit the gravesite. And you always have to play photographer because, after all, you never *knew* dead-in-law, so why would they want you posing for a family shot in front of the mausoleum?

The worst part is that only nice things are said about dead in-law. Surely, they cut someone off the road once. Told a bad joke. Or dropped a kitten. But you wouldn't know that. Everyone's too busy re-creating the myth, rewriting what a hilarious, fun-loving person they were. Dead in-law reminds you that you might be dead, but you're never gone. Even if you want to be.

### How to Combat the Dead In-Law

How do you outsmart the dead? It's hard. If you don't get on the worship train, they might haunt you. But, don't live in fear. Here are a few tricks.

1. **The Eyes Have It**
   When talking about the dearly departed always look up and say, "Uncle Charlie must be so happy looking down on us." Never look downward, which, as you know, implies that you assume dead in-law is actually rotting in hell. Just smile and

say: "I'll never forget him," but leave out the "for being such a monumental prick." Some things are better left unsaid.

2. **A-#1 Super Mourner**
   For recent deaths or gravesite visits at the cemetery, wail louder than anybody. Remember, play to the back row in the theater—we want to hear you!

3. **Philanthropy**
   Donating things to a charity in the name of dead in-laws is the most diplomatic way to deal with unwanted heirlooms. Use a flowery statement: "Mr. and Mrs. Dead In-Law's kindness, benevolence, and largesse knew no bounds. They lived for charitable acts. They would have wanted their pet dachshund to be donated to the circus."

## 2. THE DRAMA QUEEN IN-LAW

**"This isn't about you, it's about me!"**

**Favorite hobbies:** Stomping her foot, batting her eyes, sulking, hoisting up and prominently displaying "the girls" (her boobs)

**Voted in high school:** "Most Likely to Marry Up"

**Married in:** 1970, 1978, 1995, 2004 (again, to husband no. 3)

**Mistakes you made that she would never make:** Use Sun-In in your hair; date boys who aren't rich ("Why waste your time?")

**Things you have that she doesn't have:** Girlfriends

Remember the diva in your high school? The girl who played poker with the boys, took their money, and then crushed their hopes of sexual conquest—all within the fall of her freshman year? Well, about forty years ago, that was your in-law wrapping everyone around her manicured little finger: gas attendants, doormen, soccer coaches, and husbands.

Frankly, you're a little jealous. Your mother-in-law has a fifty-seven-year-old body that would shame Sigourney Weaver. *Why can't you look that amazing in white pants?* And whenever she asks her son to make a glass of lemonade, pick up socks, or take out the trash, he does it. She never has to ask twice. *Sigh.*

### Your Mother-in-Law, the Three-Year-Old

It's exciting to be your in-law. Every day delivers so much drama, and like a good hostess at her own party, she invites you into every single crisis. It's so nice of her!

Your in-law misplaces her LensCrafters eyeglass case. Boo hoo hoo. It's like she lost her favorite dolly. Of course, she pouts. Her cheeks redden. It's only ten seconds before she throws a tantrum, thusly, creating catastrophe.

Welcome to the black hole. Everything within twenty feet of your in-law gets sucked into her crisis. Suddenly, everyone is running around, trying to find her dolly. It's time to spank the baby and put her to bed, people. Say it: "You're the adult; she's the child."

Remember when you had to miss your in-law's party because of a work obligation? The conversation should have taken three minutes. Instead, your in-law's histrionics led to a 45-minute indictment of the "the work system." Eventually, you lied. You had to. Telling her your boss was violently ill from a meatball grinder wasn't true, but it was the only way to silence her and stop the rehashing of why you chose work over "family." Plain and simple, she made you do it. She's like a monkey on your back, *man*. And, you need to feed the monkey lies, *man*.

### Worst-Case Scenario: She's Southern

Cry yourself silly in the magnolias if your in-law *still* lives in the South. You've got 150 years of American history to contend with. She was groomed to live on plantations, to have genteel southern gentlemen dote on her, and to yell at the slave labor. Three things you can do: Pack your Xanax (for her, of course). Learn to make a mean mint julep. And prepare yourself to hear the following five phrases:

1. "I've never seen anything like this before in my life."
2. "Sugar plum, I'm going to have a spell. This is too much."
3. "Don't you and my son just stick together like white on rice."
4. "Aren't *transfats* just a fancy word for those women who used to be men?"
5. "The South should have won."

### You, the Competition

Your in-law refuses to believe that your husband *could possibly* love you more. Isn't she enough woman in his life? Why did he marry you? Whether you know it or not, you're caught in a love triangle, sometimes referred to as the "In-Law-Husband-You-Bermuda Triangle." Weird things happen in this triangle. Compasses lose bearings. Planes catch fire. Husbands choose dining with mother-in-law over dining with wife, because mother-in-law is upset over a fallen bird feeder.

### How to Combat the Drama Queen In-Law

Your in-law should win an Academy Award. No one can cry on the spot as she can. She makes Dame Judi Dench look like an amateur. Pulling your in-law off the stage is like pulling Bin Laden out of the Tora Bora caves. It's tough, but it can be done.

1. **Master the Art of Confusion:**
   Talk in pig latin. Answer her questions with more questions. Walk into rooms and yell at the wall. Master a few cockney phrases, such as: "Shut it, muvver, right, or I'll nick yer 'appy pills." Whatever it takes, dumbfound her. For at least a nanosecond, she'll stop thinking about herself. Checkmate!

2. **That's what whole-season DVDs are for:**
   First of all, to watch ten seasons of *ER* takes a lot of time. Now, your in-law has a purpose in life and when you talk to her, the conversation focuses on a mutually interesting topic—young George Clooney. But don't attempt to hook your in-law on DVDs if you're not A/V savvy. If her TV flickers or the sound goes out, you'll have a crisis on your hands that even hunky Dr. Ross can't fix.

3. **Get on the Gossip Train:**
   When your in-law corners you to type an e-mail for her, paint her nails, or hand her the Triscuits box while she's lying on the couch and you're four rooms away, jump on the gossip train. If your sister-in-law just found out she's pregnant (for the fifth time) and her husband remains an out-of-work actor, lob this softball to the Drama Queen! Now you avoid the mindless task she's been brewing for you since you entered her castle. She'll be on the phone with your sister-in-law in minutes.

## 3. THE ECCENTRIC IN-LAW

**"I've got unapologetic joie de vivre! And I'm broke!"**

**College:** Carleton

**Occupation:** Life coach, painter, living-by-example

**Favorite sport:** Anything noncompetitive, so that both sides can win

**Major in college:** Environmental Science; minor in Art and Ethnomusicology

**Favorite book:** *Random Acts of Kindness;* has been known to send a "friendly fax" to a stranger to start a kindness revolution

**Owns or rents?:** Rents a room in a house owned by a lovely lesbian couple

**Mistake you made that he would never make:** Offending the leader of the African Dogon tribe by drinking from the *nyama* bowl

When not busy teaching the adult continuing education class "Birds, Habitats, and Songs," your in-law is globe-trotting. He's touched more remote corners of the world than Coca-Cola. But, when he's not in Brunei, he's the stateside family photographer. His zeal for documenting your in-law family's "ancestral quest" is matched only by his love-hate relationship with biodegradable kitty litter.

### Yeah, Right, He Wouldn't Kill a Fly

Okay, so he wouldn't outright kill a fly. But he'd kill it by driving it completely crazy. This in-law controls you and your partner by being totally erratic. He zigzags. He disappears for months at a time. And sometimes he wears you thin with his refusal to use deodorant. He's the hardest opponent, because he doesn't play by the rules. And his behavior makes you worry. You can't help but feel that eventually you'll be paying for his home, electricity, and health care. That is, unless he sells that novel he's been working on.

### How to Combat the Eccentric In-Law

He's the greatest guy in the room. He's the life of the party. Learn how to ride the wave and not get sucked under.

1. **Avoid responsibility:**
   Do not co-sign loans. Do not add this in-law to your health insurance. Do not link yourself legally in *any* way. This in-law is a living liability. And, like a 185-pound anchor, he is programmed to sink. Don't get tied down.

2. **Cater to his strengths:**
   Rethink your relationship and enjoy what's great about your in-law. Instead of cursing his new obsession, say, "I'm related to a Sedona architecture expert. How wonderful!" Seek out lectures, exhibits, or nature walks that highlight your in-law's expertise.

3. **Make a list and read it aloud:**
   When your in-law's free-spirited self is downright self-destructive, list the twelve addresses he's had in the past four years, the eight jobs he's quit, and the four get-rich scams he's donated to. It may rile him, but you and your sweetie deserve time out of the dream-catcher circle.

## 4. THE SCARY IN-LAW

**"Bullshit! That ball was on the line!" Tempers flare. A tennis racket is thrown. Not at you, just near you.**

**Favorite sports:** Destroying your confidence; picking fights at your kid's T-ball game

**Things that set your in-law off:** Rain, losing, the speed limit, talking during movies, pop-up windows, people with accents

**Life motto:** "They were asking for it."

**Mistakes you made that he wouldn't make:** Not cutting in at the ski-lift line

**Things you have that he doesn't have:** Self-reflection, nap time

Your in-law would describe himself as "passionate." Unlike a scary character in a Hanna-Barbera cartoon, your in-law does not run amok yelling "Muhahahaha" at people. His rage is more subtle. He will be enjoying a tasty pistachio, until he's bumped by a woman with a stroller and starts screaming like a baboon in heat.

Your in-law flashes bicuspids in life's smallest situations. Like the time last year when he reamed out the Duane Reade clerk who wouldn't let you return an opened box of AA batteries. Or the time when your waiter forgot to bring you coffee after you politely asked twice . . . you get the point.

One day you walk up the front steps to your in-law's house and notice that something happened to the rhododendrons. They are demolished. Somehow, you simply know that "they got what they deserved" and you don't ask questions.

### Your In-Law and the Legal System

These two don't get along so well. It seems your in-law is always in the wrong place at the wrong time. He just happened to punch an undercover cop. Or he was minding his own business when an old lady came "out of nowhere" and walked directly into his golf cart. Often, your in-law will choose to represent himself before the law. But when he tries to talk himself out of a holding cell or a fine or a restraining order, he says the wrong thing. Remember when he referred to the female judge as "a dude in a skirt"?

### The Scary In-Law Is Sometimes the Racist In-Law

Your in-law claims he's not racist—after all, he added a "black" fish to his fish tank. He doesn't think it's weird to refer to his barber of ten years by race instead of by first name ("The Mexican took too much off the top"). You could chalk it up to a generation gap, but you *should* chalk it up to him being a racist. Please correct him. Please tell him that certain turns of phrase are NOT acceptable in your presence. And please tell him that "the Orient" no longer exists. Thank you.

### The Ultimate Caveat

When your in-laws are abusive—smoking around you when you're pregnant, blatantly homophobic, or painfully racist—you don't have to include them in your life. Not all relatives are happy drunks or at least healthy enough to be around. You may allow your significant other to have that bond, but you need not get involved. We can only hope that in this case, your sweetie—the proverbial apple—fell far from the tree. Very, very far.

## How to Combat the Scary In-Law

Sometimes your in-law is gentle as a lamb. Sometimes he's a tiger. He really needs a mood ring. Isolate his trigger points and you're golden; otherwise, you're just in his way.

1. **Abstain:**
   It's not a good idea to get stinking drunk with your in-law. You could become involved in some flashback sequence where he thinks you're "that chick" who wronged him once in a Trader Joe's parking lot.

2. **Know the chink in the armor:**
   You're at a Chicago Cubs game and a fan yells a disparaging remark about the pitcher. Your in-law, a lifelong Cubs fan, ignites. Life is rocky with this in-law, but if you isolate and avoid the hot buttons (e.g., Chicago Deep Dish vs. New York Pizza) you can skip over life's potholes unscathed.

3. **Stay with the group:**
   Fly-fishing in the wilderness sounds great, just not with this in-law. Thinking about hiking and "escaping" civilization for a while? Think again. Why on earth would you want to hang out with a ticking time bomb *away* from other people? Would you drink prune juice on an empty stomach and drive away from a bathroom? And, please don't go to places with your in-law where cell phone service falters. Remember there's safety in numbers. Such as 9-1-1.

## 5. THE MANIPULATOR IN-LAW

**"Whatever you say is fine, dear.
But you know how your father can be."**

**Favorite hobbies:** Giving the silent treatment, cleaning the house, cooking, folding the laundry, plotting, leaving passive-aggressive phone messages

**College:** Her accomplishments are her kids

**Where you can find her:** The suburbs

**She's most likely to:** Stare at someone at the gym until they become so uncomfortable they give her the treadmill

Not to be confused with the Drama Queen, the Manipulator looks out for numero uno—her son—and brings a more stealthy approach to the table. The Manipulator *is* the all-American mom. She lives for her family and she'll never let you forget it so long as she's alive. She's allowed everyone to walk all over her for years, and she's totally okay with it. She didn't complain when they repaved the driveway, and they accidentally paved over her. She didn't make a fuss! Not her style!

This in-law controls with guilt. But her powers weaken when directly confronted. That's why she's evasive. Somehow, you find yourself catering to her, reading cryptic body language, and translating double-talk, all to surmise that she'd rather eat chicken than fish. Sometimes you're lucky and you find out *exactly* how your mother-in-law feels via her proxy—your brother-in-law. This woman pits family against each other like the mastermind of an illegal cockfighting ring. It's just her little way of making you feel horrible, sad, rejected, and generally agitated. Did you want butter with that or are you still trying to lose some weight?

**Phrase she works into everyday conversation:** "Well, I'm not going to say anything, because you're the one who has to live with the decision . . ."

**Her favorite day:** Her son's birthday. This is a 24-hour period of time when immediate family celebrates her son—her greatest creation.

**Her worst nightmare:** Being identified by her daughter-in-law as the Manipulator

## How to Combat the Manipulator In-Law

You need tools—really sharp tools that puncture. Your in-law is like a Mylar balloon. One "pop" and that sunny party-face will droop, unless she Botoxed, which you know she didn't because that's just too much money spent on her, although they do have gift certificates. Hint. Hint.

1. **Disarm her and win allies:**
   Compliment her profusely. Shower her with attention. Shine your spotlight on this wallflower. Make this "unsung hero" sing a different tune. Go out on a limb and grocery shop or do the laundry for her. She'll be indebted, and it might give her extremely long-suffering husband a break. Not that he matters much, but at least now there's someone else on your side.

2. **Change the dynamic:**
   Mothers-in-law aren't passive-aggressive with everyone in their lives. Crash her bridge club. Cards, alcohol, and cucumber sandwiches are centuries-old truth serums. Oh, how the girls will gab. See what your in-law is like when she's not disappointed in her family. For these few hours, she is not your in-law. You are not her daughter-in-law. You're a card-playing shark who takes her money. Revel in it.

3. **Become aggressive-aggressive:**
Unearth the passive cover-up. Instead of quietly drowning in the pressurized tide pool of guilt, stand your ground. Your in-law says, "My other daughter-in-law always picks me up at the airport. I never take an airport shuttle." You respond, "So what you're saying is that I'm a bad daughter-in-law?" If she's mad, make her say it! The emperor has no clothes!

## 6. THE IN-LAW YOU LIKE BETTER THAN YOUR OWN PARENT

**You got the short end of the stick growing up, and finally, you have a brand-new set of parents to disappoint.**

**Hobbies:** Golfing and cooking (yours are caddying and eating)

**College:** The college you attended or wish you had attended

**Phrase they say:** "We love you like our own daughter."

**Their favorite person:** You, the Dali Lama, Homer Simpson

**Their worst nightmare:** For you to be unhappy, hungry, or unloved

**Life motto:** "We don't want to cramp your style!"

Congratulations on winning the in-law jackpot. Your in-laws are perfect. They are:

- Entertaining and eccentric when you're waiting in line at the DMV
- Knowledgeable and worldly when you want to expand your horizons and learn curling

- Gentle when you scrape your knee
- Excited to eat at Denny's when you crave onion rings
- Supportive when you need assurance that filing a complaint against your boss is the right thing to do
- Amazing role models for marriage
- Understanding when you're moody with "Aunt Flo"

You're on cloud nine looking down at the rest of us on cloud eight. But have you silenced the lurking doubt that maybe ( just maybe) with more time, these in-laws could blossom into parents from hell? No, of course not. Sorry to suggest that.

The truth is that you've had your entire life to be irritated by your own brood. There's so much history there. You haven't waited long enough to let your new in-laws annoy you. You're still dazed by the shiny new packaging. It won't be long before your in-laws are gunning past rest stops when you have to pee or lying to waitresses about your age to get kids' meal prices just like ma and pa used to do. Inevitably, your in-laws will dirty their clean slate, kick over their pedestal, and ask you to prepare four dozen deviled eggs for a family picnic this afternoon. It's just a matter of time.

### How to Combat the In-law You Like Better Than Your Own Parent

The word *combat* feels a little strong here. Really, what you want to do is "maintain." How do you keep the rose-tinted glasses on?

1. **Short visits:**

   Don't overstay, because there's a chance your in-laws might soil their golden diaper. Make it short and sweet. If you hear your in-laws arguing, leave in the middle of the night. Or if they begin to negatively review your favorite book, just excuse yourself mid-meal. They're your BFF, so you can return later when it's over. They'll understand. They always do.

2. **A memory box:**
   Fill your home with memorabilia of your in-law family. Frame the street carnival sketch of you and your in-laws at the Lincoln Memorial. Hang the Kmart family portraits. Carry around the napkin your father-in-law used last week to figure out the dinner tip. Keep everything, because looking at them is a shot in the arm when you need it. You in-law junkie, you.

3. **Return to your roots:**
   Remind yourself of the horror of your own family. They often forget you exist, let alone that you moved out of the house seven years ago (yet last night, they knocked on your bedroom door to tell you dinner was ready). Whatever the case, you want out all over again. It's like pushing a bruise—it's always going to hurt.

## 7. THE PERFECTIONIST IN-LAW

**"This is how I suggest you do it, because it's right."**

**College:** Harvard

**Refers to your college as:** The Harvard of the West

**Degrees:** M.D., Ph.D., and J.D.

**Number of lovers before getting married:** Four (the math club was horny)

**Things you have that they don't:** A winning video on *America's Funniest Home Videos* of your friend accidentally falling off a ladder
**Car they drive:** The high horse they rode in on

Your in-laws really *are* that impressive. They work for the UN and eliminated polio in Senegal. They speak eight languages fluently, while you still have trouble with transitive verbs. And they have "dear friends" who live in Laos, Croatia, New Zealand, Morocco, India, Germany, and Nova Scotia, while most of your friends still live at home. Not to mention they make their own gnocchi, sold paintings to San Francisco MOMA's permanent collection, and bowl a 300 game, consistently.

Did you feel like a loser when your father-in-law retired from a long career behind a desk on Wall Street, suddenly took up tennis, and became a touring pro? Yeah, I bet you did.

### You, the Crackhead, Married Their Son

You thought you looked adorable the other day when you lunched with your in-laws. It was a sunny day. The food was terrific. The outdoor bistro delightful. You mustered up the courage to celebrate a new development in your life: your recent decision to leave your heinous job in banking for a more fulfilling career as a florist. Instead of sharing in your joy, your in-laws went silent; their posture stiffened. Their daughter-in-law had just stepped off the path to success. Now, she was a wayward soul, probably fired for gross incompetence, whose only future was making floral arrangements out of trash for maximum security prisoners.

Your in-laws tap into your insecurity with the dexterity of a spine surgeon. How can people be so *perfect*? They never make mistakes. When you told them that funny story about the time you ran out of gas and Bono happened to drive by, picked you up, and bought you beers for five hours, they focused on why you didn't fill the gas tank when it went below half full, and who drove home after all those beers, anyway?

### Dark Master of the Backhanded Compliment

Below are five typical phrasings in which your perfect in-laws prove that they are even more perfect than you. Welcome to the emotional roller coaster of praise and putdown.

1. "I'm so excited to see your performance! I'm getting there early, because I don't want to miss the overture like you did when we took you to *Tosca*."
2. "Your garden looks terrific! But why spend money on annuals and not perennials? I was more frugal at your age."
3. "Former President Clinton is giving a quote for my latest book. How's your job these days?"
4. "Can I use your bathroom for a second? Is it clean? Because I know how you kids live!"
5. "Oh, my! You cut your hair! It's looks wonderful. Thank God you took care of it. I kept telling myself there was a pretty face under there."

### How to Combat the Perfectionist In-Law

Dare to attempt the impossible. Impress them. You can stump the debater, outrun the marathoner, and outseason the chef. How? Flattery. It will get you everywhere. So, raise the roof because the impossibly large ego of your in-laws will inflate even more.

1. **Relate to them on their own level:**
   The minute something great happens to you, call your in-laws and let them know they are the first people you called, because being #1 in your life is more important to them than your nomination for a Fulbright.

2. **The best gift:**
   A bobble-head dog on the dashboard makes you laugh for hours, but it's not right for their Mercedes. Instead, give them a gift that illustrates your financial savvy. Buy them stock in Coca-Cola. It can never go down.

3. **Memorize:**
   Commit to the tip of your tongue the capitals of every nation ending in "-stan" and the name of at least one current or former ruler. This will arm you for the many dinner conversations with your in-laws and their foreign ambassador/ Olympic Committee guests.

## In-Laws: The Good, the Bad, and the Ugly

Do you feel like you inherited Mr. and Mrs. Very Annoying? Just remember, it can always be worse. There are some horrible, terrible, miserable in-laws to have. And, in case you can't think of them, here's a little chart to tack up on the refrigerator and gaze upon in your darkest moments.

| Worst in-law to have | Your in-laws are better because they don't . . . | At least your in-laws won't say . . . |
|---|---|---|
| Dick Cheney | Smell like sulfur from their repeated trips to hell. | "Sorry, I shot you in the face with a hunting rifle. My mistake!" |
| Oprah | Dine with Dr. Phil. | "You go girl." |
| Medusa | Turn you into stone, when you look them in the eyes. | "Fetch me some mice to feed my hair." |
| Blackbeard | Steal from you and bury your engagement ring in the sand. | "Will you be honeymooning in Hispaniola this year? We know a great brothel." |
| The Professor from *X-Men* | Read your mind. | "This matter is of grave importance. Could you just wheel me over to my (thinking) chamber, the Cerbro?" |
| Kim Jong-il | Spend 50 percent of your household income on nuclear proliferation. | "The Sea of Japan is mine! All mine!!" |
| Martha Stewart | Shun you for not knowing how to craft marzipan farm animals. | "You must have misunderstood what I meant by medium rare." |
| Bruce Willis | Try to sleep with you. | "Let's go back to my place. Are you too young to remember *Die Hard*?" |
| Santa Claus | Get you slipper socks for Christmas then silently mouth the word *naughty* at you. | "Goddamn lazy midgets! You can't get good help these days!" |
| Lance Armstrong | Wake you for a friendly bike ride at the crack of dawn. | "That's nice, but until you've won the tour seven times, we don't have much to talk about." |

Congratulations on learning the personalities of your in-laws. Now you're ready to tackle the tough question: Does *everyone* in his family act this way? (Hint: they often do.)

Good luck.

# the in-law family tree

## How your sweetie grew up in it, fell far out of it, and sometimes returns to its roots

EXCERPT FROM THE AUTHOR'S DIARY:

*My mother-in-law is a talented Beat poet. She just doesn't know it. The other day, she stopped me in the kitchen to recite one of her finest:*

*Do you know you have potato salad in the fridge?*
*Why do you have potato salad in the fridge?*
*Are you going to eat this potato salad?*
*Can I eat it?*

*Why is the recycling on the back porch?*
*Didn't it used to be in the basement?*
*Do you like having it on the back porch?*
*Will you move it to the basement someday?*
*When?*

*Do you want the peaches I brought all the way from Georgia?*
*Does my son want one of the peaches I brought from Georgia?*

*Does my grandson want a peach?*
*Did I tell you that I brought them all the way from Georgia?*

*Beat poetry is for the birds. I just want my house back.*

## The Best Apple in the Barrel

There are many branches of the in-law family tree, and you're in love with one of them. Like a grand aspen grove, your beloved is connected to a root system of hundreds of relatives. When one tree grows sick and infested with tent caterpillars, it affects them all. That's family.

So, you've fallen for the smartest, sexiest, funniest person in the world. The one and only! And, you're about to meet five other people who share his DNA. They might look like him and they might talk like him. Or they might have no idea what he is saying and look to you for answers.

## Nature vs. Nurture

When you observe your "better half" in the context of his family, it's like stepping inside *The Matrix*. You begin to understand how the family system functions. Admittedly, this isn't as cool as battling the Machines and jumping off buildings with Morpheus and Neo, but this new worldview of your partner is a valuable tool for developing your relationship.

A lightbulb blinks on in your head. You say, "Aha! That's where he gets it from" because you learn that his annoying habits—talking in the background while you're on the phone, bouncing checks, and hyperventilating on planes—were acquired from his annoying family. Or, "Huh? I have no idea where he gets it from" because you and your in-laws are equally confused by your partner's new two-week obsession with militant veganism.

### The Nature Trail

First, examine the physical characteristics passed down in your beloved's family lineage:

- **The bump on the bridge of the nose:** Your sister-in-law doesn't have it; she took care of that "deviated septum" in high school.
- **The ring around the bald spot:** Could they be crop circles? Are aliens saying hi?
- **The very, very tall gene:** Who are these giants with their large hands? And where do they find clothes that fit?
- **The very, very loud gene:** They say your name—"Ma-ri-ahh!"—and your ears bleed.
- **The connected earlobes:** Your in-laws are the missing genetic link between fish and man.
- **The sweaty gene:** It's 11 AM and there have been four costume changes.

### Nurture, a.k.a. Habits That *Can* Be Broken

Next, you identify the learned personality traits and behaviors. Quickly it becomes clear which annoying habits your sweetie picked up from his college roommate and which were passed from his parents. Now you know that the ravenous frenzy he engages in every night at dinner—the inhalation of an entire breadbasket, large pizza, or Caesar salad in four minutes with his mouth open, occasionally gasping for air—is his family's teaching. *Sigh.*

Only with new blood in the family (i.e., yours) will such habits evolve. In the meantime, everyone in your in-law family:

- Believes they must deliver their own personal news about car repairs, clothing purchases, and dating life like CNN—live, in person, and always in the moment. And replay it over and over again throughout the day.
- Never orders a meal in a restaurant that "they could easily prepare at home," which explains your partner's clucking disapproval of your grilled cheese entree.
- Books airline tickets for all family trips one week ahead because "who likes to feel tied down?"
- Goes hog-wild for birthdays and floods your mailbox with invitations for yet another celebration—this time it's for third cousin Miles, who's turning sixty-three. (People, this isn't an age that's divisible by five! Let it be!)
- Sets their clocks ahead by random amounts of time and still arrive late.
- Greets you with open-mouth kisses (what was *that*—did Grandad just lick your face?).

## Aristotle's *Poetics* and the Importance of Backstory

Before you met your in-laws, you were watching a made-for-TV movie of your beloved's life. Now, after interacting with the family, you're living the full details of the book. You have narrative background, multiple plot lines, and compelling supporting characters. Sizing up your father-in-law and grandfather-in-law, you can visualize what your partner will look like at age fifty and at age eighty. Aside from the Amazonian nose hairs, it almost looks promising. The Thanksgiving turducken will also be no surprise. Nor will be the group sing-a-long to: "It's a chicken in a duck in a turkey in the oven!"

Of course, there are things about your significant other that you would love to change. It's frustrating that your partner refuses to buy anything for full price. Then you meet his family and they show you the "ships in the bottle" they bought for 40 percent off! Can you believe it?—40 percent below sticker price? Know at that moment that for the rest of your lives together, you will be returning items and yelling at store managers because "no sale is ever final."

By identifying which habits are entrenched in his family, you can choose your battles more effectively. A time-worn tradition will be impossible to change; a new one is surmountable.

## Deep Roots

Every male member of your sweetie's family glues his ass to the couch for Redskins games. An autosomal dominant Redskins gene has been passed through the generations and your man has it, too.

So, you can bet that on fall Sundays between the hours of 1 PM and 6 PM your in-laws will stink up the living room. You'll live a happier life if you don't assume the Herculean task of changing this habit. Instead, leave the house and don't look back. Call your best lady friends and know that for sixteen weeks a year, your partner will use your red lipstick as face paint. Breathe and say: "Just fifteen, fourteen, thirteen weeks more . . ."

You know this book is a safe space. Vent, dear reader. Expose those habits to the light by writing your partner and his family's idiosyncrasies in the spaces below.

*For example: It's bizarre that my entire in-law family* ***annually drives 15 hours to a vacation rental on Lake Michigan. Why not fly people?! Gas is so expensive!***

I don't like it when my partner and his family do this ________
__________________________________________________.

And, this ______________. Okay, and this ________________.

Ah, doesn't that feel better?

### The Young Sapling

Tired of eating "spicy" peanut butter sandwiches, "south-of-the-border" yogurts, and "three-alarm" pancakes? Your partner's homegrown tomatillo sauce obsession is killing you. Challenge it. He can do shots of Tabasco all he wants at work, in the car, or at the bank, but at home with you and your irritable bowel, he's likely to lay off the hot sauce in favor of some sweet lovin'.

There are family ties that bind, and then there are those that threaten to cut your beloved off from the outside world. If a learned family habit proves more destructive than "three-alarm nachoism"—such as an addiction to alcohol or gambling—with your guidance and support, your partner can overcome these troubling traits. He is lucky to have finally adopted a new, healthy family member to mimic when the family tree beckons. With you building a sweet rope-swing off one branch, he'll get the balance he needs.

## Family Dynamics: Three Bears, Wicked Stepsisters, Seven Dwarfs—Every Family Has Its Pecking Order

Your significant other's role in his family tribe greatly defines his character. Open your eyes to the power rankings. Which one are you dating?

### The Black Sheep

You've fallen in love with the family outcast. Sure, your partner was a child violin prodigy, graduated medical school at age sixteen, was named this year's most civic-minded, charitable, all-around best person in the country. He still can't do anything right in his family's eyes.

You learn details about "the good kid" in the family. And, the good kid (a.k.a. your brother-in-law) is a complete idiot. Nope, it's not weird that the good kid spends all of his time blogging about fantasy basketball and your honey spends all his time at a real job. Doesn't matter!

Don't worry about loving the undesired. There are many benefits to dating the blackest of the black sheep:

- Don't like your in-laws? No problem. Your partner has ensured that you will never have to deal with them. You get away with murder because your in-laws have already written you off. They assume there's a trash bag filled with human heads in the trunk of your Saturn—I mean, you're dating *him*, right?
- On the flip side, your lover has set the bar so low that with every gracious gesture they not only think you're amazing, but you're bridging the family gap with each sweet thank-you note. Thanks for bringing their baby back from the dark side.
- You can go wherever you want for the holidays. They don't expect him to come home ever since that year he was surgically repairing cleft-palate children in Rwanda and missed Christmas. What a grinch.

## The Golden Child

You've snatched your in-law family's shining glory and they want him back. Or at the very least, they want to touch him, smell him, and smother him every single day.

Often you feel like the third wheel, or the fifth. That's because you are. And your darkest fears? They're true. Your in-law family *doesn't* think you're good enough, smart enough, or attractive enough for their baby. In their eyes, you're not capable of loving your man as much as they do. You worry that they're right.

Seeing him worshipped like the Sun King can make your stomach turn. Here's how to deal with your in-laws when dating the family celebrity:

- If your in-laws feel the need to rush over and coddle your sweetie when he catches a cold, establish clear boundaries. You aren't traveling the Oregon Trail in the 1860s! He does not have consumption! And thanks to your progressive employer, he does have health insurance. Who's taking care of baby now? Ha!
- Allow your partner alone time with his family. They desperately need it. He might need it, too. And how many women can run their hands through his hair at one time anyway?
- It's fine if he is insanely loyal to his fan base, if you clearly come first. He can sign all of the autographs he wants, so long as he leaves the party when you're ready to go. Be Trudie Styler to his Sting. When you say "Jump!" he should say: "For how long—er—how high?"

## The Guilty Child

He takes great care of you, but he also takes great care of his family. Are you ready to be sucked into bizarre in-law events?

We're talking about midnight excursions to fix air-conditioning units, giving up weekends to clean in-law garages, and bailing his sister and her new "boyfriend" out of jail. It's not easy to sympathize with Mr. Dutiful and Doting, but here are a few tips:

- As your in-laws age and their behaviors become crystal clear, learn what your partner's expectations are regarding the health and financial care of his family. Talking through these scenarios will curb any irrational responses to life's hardest decisions. If relocating your brother-in-law to your living room is not an option, speak up before he loses his job. Again.
- Take the weight off your partner's shoulders. Relieve him of his guilt when his sister has a bikini wax massacre and needs someone to add fresh cubes to her ice bath. Be his right-hand man.
- Remind him that even Atlas needs a Caribbean vacation—*once in a while*. Everyone deserves to check out of life now and again. Assure him that his family will be better off if he recharges his engines. With renewed vigor, he'll be able to wallpaper their mud room in record time.

### The Competitive Sibling

There is no second place for your partner. Normally sublime with you, your sweetie's competitive side gets drawn into "the family game." Life with your in-laws is black and white. There are only winners and those pitiful "losers" who lost.

You and yours will always have the larger diamond ring, hardier snow tires, more fabulous vacations, and smarter children than anyone else in his family. Whatever the competition, you will compete, conquer, and flaunt. Got it?

- What are the stakes? If it's a harmless contest, accept it. But once paintball takes an ugly turn, pull the rip cord. There's no need for your sweetie to engage in weekend warrior competitions, throwing his back in "simulated combat" to avoid being a "crybaby who wants his mommy."
- Stay aligned with your partner. Mum's the word about the real reason behind his black eye. No, it wasn't that he pushed past 300-pound defenders to score a winning touchdown for the office intramural championship. He slipped in the shower. After he used your girly moisturizing body rinse.
- Help your love become a champion. Flaunt your sorority-honed skills at the family badminton tournament. You're a ringer! Victory never tasted so sweet, until you slam a birdie into your competitive sister-in-law's unibrow. It's like a target. A large magnetic target. Yikes.

## Drawing the Family Tree

Crafting your own in-law family tree takes dedication, patience, and a lot of free time—that's what "sick days" are for. Visual aids clarify the branches of the in-law family tree. You have too many in-laws named Gus, Nick, and Jimmy to fully grasp who's who. You need a bird's-eye view of the situation. So grab a ruler, some colored pencils, and get charting!

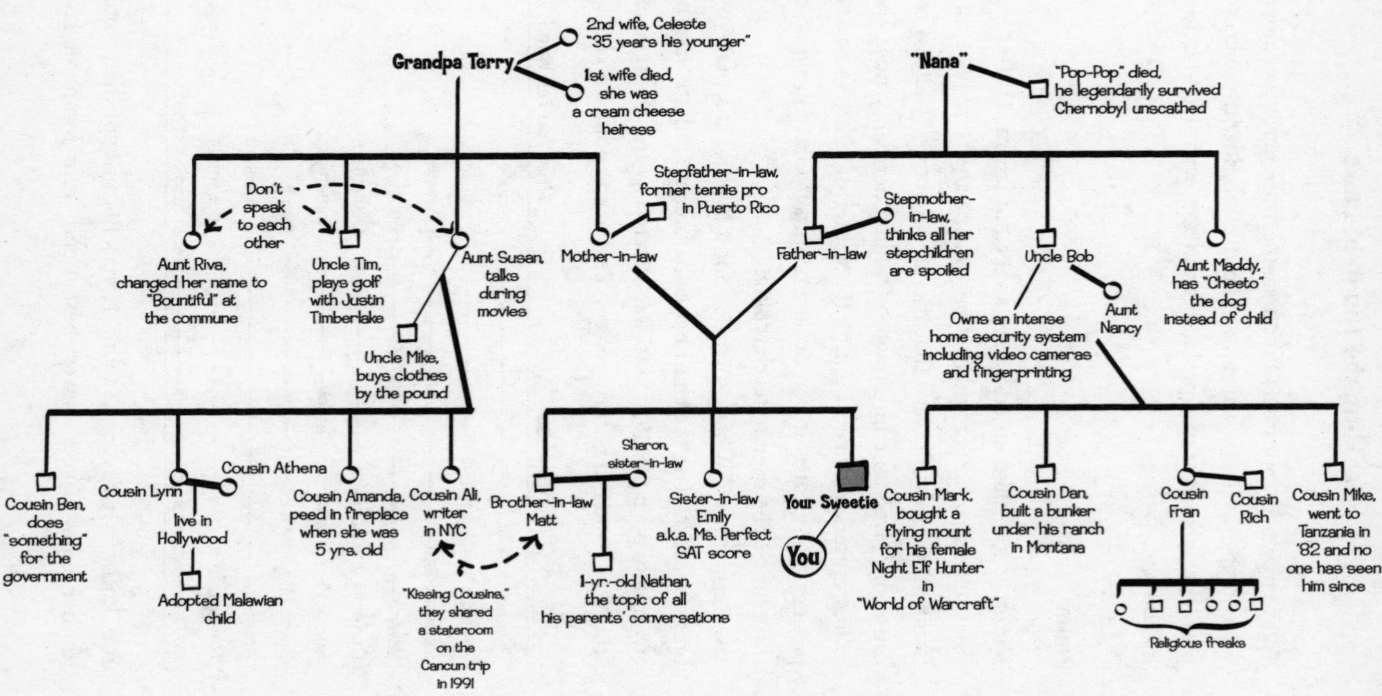
The In-Law Family Tree
Grandpa Terry
2nd wife, Celeste "35 years his younger"
1st wife died, she was a cream cheese heiress
"Nana"
"Pop-Pop" died, he legendarily survived Chernobyl unscathed
Don't speak to each other
Aunt Riva, changed her name to "Bountiful" at the commune
Uncle Tim, plays golf with Justin Timberlake
Aunt Susan, talks during movies
Uncle Mike, buys clothes by the pound
Mother-in-law
Stepfather-in-law, former tennis pro in Puerto Rico
Father-in-law
Stepmother-in-law, thinks all her stepchildren are spoiled
Uncle Bob
Aunt Nancy
Owns an intense home security system including video cameras and fingerprinting
Aunt Maddy, has "Cheeto" the dog instead of child
Cousin Ben, does "something" for the government
Cousin Lynn
Cousin Athena
live in Hollywood
Adopted Malawian child
Cousin Amanda, peed in fireplace when she was 5 yrs. old
Cousin Ali, writer in NYC
"Kissing Cousins," they shared a stateroom on the Cancun trip in 1991
Brother-in-law Matt
Sharon, sister-in-law
1-yr.-old Nathan, the topic of all his parents' conversations
Sister-in-law Emily a.k.a. Ms. Perfect SAT score
Your Sweetie
You
Cousin Mark, bought a flying mount for his female Night Elf Hunter in "World of Warcraft"
Cousin Dan, built a bunker under his ranch in Montana
Cousin Fran
Cousin Rich
Religious freaks
Cousin Mike, went to Tanzania in '82 and no one has seen him since

## Tackling the Tough In-Laws

You've mapped your tree. Of course, there are family members who stand out like a bad home hair-dye job. Identify who's a problem *before* they're a problem and learn what to do before it's too late.

### Nana

She may look like an adorable, sweet human raisin. But she rules with a ruthless mind grip on your partner and his entire family. You can't tell Nana that you are an actress/waitress because she saved an entire town by boiling her panty hose and selling erasers for 2 cents during the winter of 1927. She was a pioneer. So, what is it you do again, missy? Oh, you work in computers? She used to teach typing!

Remember, "What do you do for a living?" is a make-or-break question. Use the chart below before you talk to Nana or any in-law born pre-1930 who was affected by the Depression, "the War," and did not have easy access to the polio vaccine.

| Your Job | What You Tell Nana |
|---|---|
| Psychiatrist——> | Doctor |
| Sketch comedy actress——> | Producer |
| Sports writer——> | Lawyer |
| Lawyer——> | Rabbi |
| Currently unemployed——> | Computers |
| Senior Vice President for Target——> | Homemaker |
| Brand Manager for Crest——> | Dentist |
| Accountant——> | Accountant |
| Manager of Kinko's——> | Accountant |
| Ph.D. candidate for gender studies——> | In medical school |

You know what's great about Nana? Because of her, your mother-in-law is your newest best friend. Your mother-in-law has a mother-in-law who drives her crazy. Nana has forged an alliance between you two. Together you deflect her criticisms and running commentary about pecan pie and diverticulitis.

### The Materialistic Brother-in-Law with Influence

He's a gigolo who's maxed out his parents' credit card. But he's the apple of your in-laws' eyes. So you should overlook his smug white belts, leather shoes, and sunglasses, because ten seconds after you're out the front door and down the driveway, he'll tell them what he thinks of you and it's forever etched in stone.

Ingratiate yourself to this spoiled brat by buying him things: Cuban cigars, Lacoste shirts, and lap dances. Or align yourself by being his "fashion police" partner at your next family gathering. Channel your inner bitch and arrest Aunt Anne for her pleated denim shorts. Poor Aunt Anne. She didn't deserve a $50 fine, but your brother-in-law needs to know you're serious.

### The Uncle-in-Law Who Hits on You

He pinches your ass, and not in that "sportsmanship kind of way." He gazes not at your eyes, but eyes twelve inches south. Face it—he's the shirtless, sockless guy at the gym who winks at you after your set on the hamstring machine and says, "Need a spotter?"

It's nice that he always mentions how gorgeous you are. Thanks for the compliment, perv! But sorry, my dance card is full. To truly combat this in-law, play to his low level. Become tight with his ex-girlfriend and learn that Mister Creepy is not so well proportioned down below. When he sees you with her, he'll know that *you* know that although he is happy to see you, it's just a dumbbell in his pocket. Literally. It's a dumbbell.

### The Scorned Sister-in-Law

She graduated from Harvard where she and your sweetie were best friends. She's smart, stylish, and would be your best gal pal if you didn't take up so much of her brother's time.

If she's not directly combative with you (which she is 50 percent of the time), she drives your significant other CRAZY to get his attention. After seeing her, you can't climb into bed without hearing: "Can you believe my sister said that? What gives her the right to criticize? I mean, just look at her life . . ."

The only way to mollify this attention-whore is to acknowledge her existence immediately on arrival and be ready with anecdotes/observations that tout her superiority in relation to yourself, her brother, and everyone else in the room. Feel free to say:

- "Thank God you're here!"
- "You're so right. Brenda was robbed at the Peach Pit. I missed that episode."
- "We never got to finish our conversation about your solution to peace in the Middle East . . ."
- "I would never think of combining a fringed leather belt, an orange skirt, and Tretorn sneakers, but you pull it off!"
- "You so have a dancer's body."

### The Harbinger of Bad News In-Law

Hey, did you know that so-and-so was going blind? Or that 227 acres in Colorado are in flames *right now*? With this life-of-the-party in-law, you know that all passengers aboard flight 182 heading to Corsica died midair. Fun! Hey, he's keepin' it real. So real that you want to put your head in the oven. And after you do, this in-law will announce it proudly to everyone.

Always be ready with a dose of cheer. "Hey, I heard koalas

have finally been taken off the watch list for endangered species!" or "My mom's tumor is benign—how great is that?" Chances are you'll have the last word in that scenario.

### The Religious In-Law

You can't escape. It's been twenty minutes and you've been stuck talking to the proselytizing cult-leader-freak in your in-law family. Expect to hear:

- "Do you accept Jesus Christ to be your personal savior today?"
- "Live with me on the kibbutz. The rest of the family hasn't embraced God, but I can tell you're different."
- "We don't eat meat. We love animals. But go ahead and gnaw on the raw flesh of a senselessly murdered cow. Really, go ahead."
- "I prepare myself by fasting. Join me. Now."
- "If you want peace and light in your life, be a Buddhist. If you don't, you can walk a path of ignorance. You're free to make bad choices."

Thank the religious in-law for the dogma and for playing the "let's not make eye contact even though we are seated directly opposite each other" game after you rebuff his religious offers.

Why does this in-law make waves so big he can part the sea? You can show respect for your in-law's traditions, without actually joining them. If your in-law pressures you by saying: "My wife wasn't Catholic either, but she converted," respond with: "You're lucky that it was so simple for you. [My partner] and I hope to blend our different backgrounds into our new home." Then give him a dreidel.

**"Morsels," the In-Law Pet that Bites**

Nobody seems to mind that your in-laws' dog isn't house-trained and bites because "he doesn't like men." Great yogi masters teach about accepting that which you cannot change. Open your mind's eye. You will find the animal friend has more rights and clout than you. So pack a box of Claritin and some doggie treats because "Morsels" is on the prowl.

Repeat these meditation chants before entering your in-laws' household.

**I accept** that there will be dog hair on my brand-new Michael Kors sweater.

**I accept** that "Marzipan," the 100-pound golden retriever, will climb on my lap and attempt to nurse.

**I accept** that the puppy pees when I startle her in the kitchen and it's my fault.

**I accept** that "Rex" will knock my cell phone off the coffee table, sending it skidding across the floor and under the couch.

**I accept** that all conversations no matter how important will be interrupted by "Oh my god! That's the cutest thing" and "Did you see that?"

**I accept** that they cannot drive me to the airport because they are driving "Freckles" to the groomer.

**I accept** that their cat scratches, hides in my closet, and sleeps in my suitcase.

**I accept** that my burning eyes, constant sneezing, and swollen sinuses result from my own genetic weakness.

**I accept** that there may be one redeeming quality—*somewhere*—in a pet bird.

If you are a pet person, it can strongly work in your favor. Rescuing "Simon," the frantic shih tzu, from his imminent death on the other side of the electrical fence or saving "Hot Pants" from beneath the radiator is the most direct path to sainthood. However, there's no need to risk your life to impress your in-laws.

Offer to drive "Stella Blue" to her chemotherapy appointment. While you're at Dr. Felder's office answering questions about her food and beverage preferences, don't bother answering your cell phone. How do you explain what you're doing to friends? You can't! Of course, you have better things to do than suck on free bone-shaped breath mints and read *Dog Fancy,* but do it for the love of the dog, and earn the love of your in-laws.

### The Divorced In-Law

Your in-law had a miserable marriage and now it's your problem, too. Balancing which in-law to see, when, and for how long is exhausting. Without a doubt, the "other" in-law feels snubbed.

Clearly, there's pressure to visit all in-laws equally. This would work just fine if all things were equal. Someone lives in Hong Kong. Another lives in your town. So, you rotate through the holidays to visit each of them, plus your folks. That's *three* sets of parents to rotate through. Your own family is bound to feel the shaft since technically you're spending more time with the in-laws—66 percent of the time, in fact.

Dealing with divorced in-laws is like juggling bottles of nitroglycerin. You never know which one is going to explode. The only way to handle these scenarios is to communicate. Let each in-law know that you're trying to split time equally. That's all you can do. If they really protest, suggest slicing yourself into thirds. Would that help?

It's never a great idea to get caught counting the days, hours, and minutes you owe each family member. But if you do, here's a chart to help, because all time is not equal.

**How Much Is Your In-Law Time Worth?**

| In-Law Visit | Days Spent | Days Earned | Justification |
|---|---|---|---|
| Holiday with grandparents-in-law in Key West | 5 | 3 | You spend most of your time sucking down mojitos and gawking at the glitterati. This hardly counts as work. |
| Visit uncle-in-law in San Quentin | 1 | 4 | Prisoners lick the glass at you while your partner catches up with Uncle Louie. |
| Memorial Day weekend at brother-in-law's house | 2 | 1 | You drink home-brewed corn beer and light roman candle firecrackers. Easy. |
| Attend "revival meeting" with sister-in-law | 1/12 of a day (2 hrs.) | 2 | You sing many rousing rounds to "Kumbaya," and your clothes reek of incense. |
| Visit nana-in-law in hospice center in Eugene, Ore. | 2 | 5 | Grandma's got only six months left. You lend a shoulder to sobbing in-laws and bring donuts. You are an angel. |
| Meeting in-laws for first time in Buffalo, N.Y. (they liked the old girlfriend better) | 4 | 8,000 | A freak blizzard leaves you trapped inside with no electricity and a family full of Yahtzee-Nazis. |
| Hosting mother-in-law in NYC | 1 | 5 | She forces you to attend *The Vagina Monologues* and drink with the cast afterward. |

Mapping your in-laws doesn't just mean literally drawing your family tree and planning your vacation days among them. It means mapping the geographic distances, too. Normally, it doesn't matter that Harry, your in-law cousin twice removed, is a social animal. That is, until he moves next door.

4

# location, location, location

**Where your in-laws live directly affects your social calendar and therapy bills.**

EXCERPT FROM THE AUTHOR'S DIARY:

*Just as I closed the door to my therapist's office, I spotted my in-laws. I fumbled with the door to get back in, but it was locked. I quickly wiped my nose, tossed my crumpled tissue into a plant, patted my eyes, and smiled broadly. "Hi, you guys! What a surprise! My eyes get so irritated after seeing the ophthalmologist." I then realized that the last hour of Freudian analysis was unnecessary. My in-laws were the midget fish-people with braces in my dream. I buzzed my therapist's doorbell, mumbling something about forgotten eye drops. Clearly, I need to move. Or start sessions twice a week.*

## Sharing Planet Earth with Your In-Laws

Two hundred million years ago, New York State was attached to Morocco in Pangaea. This means that at one point in history, we were all technically within walking distance of our in-laws. Then a series of earthquakes occurred, tectonic plates shifted, and landmasses parted. Sighs of relief were breathed.

Regardless of where on the map your in-laws live—across the street or across the ocean—their relative distance to you affects your relationship with them.

## A Plane Flight Away

Having in-laws that live in India might seem wonderfully far away until they move into your apartment for monsoon season. I mean, what's the point of visiting the States unless it's for four weeks? Right?

For the other forty-eight weeks, you and your sweetie are an independent family living on an island of uninterrupted bliss. Most of your in-law communication is via phone and e-mail. That is, until the big visit. Then, from the moment the 747 jumbo jet touches down until the flight attendant announces the in-flight movie options on the return trip, it's a whirlwind of dinners, tours, and extended family celebrations.

> "My Bangladeshi in-laws live with me for two months of the year. Yes, this is great 'quality time' but as a medical resident, I make my already busy life, busier. I take extra overnight calls. I volunteer for early morning reports. I basically disappear to escape my own apartment!"
>
> TANIA, PHILADELPHIA

Don't have international, globe-trotting in-laws? Maybe your in-laws live in Coral Gables, Florida, and visit New England for only a week because "it's too cold to stay any longer." It's still as if a comet crashed into your life, burned through your refrigerator, and obliterated everything you saved on Tivo.

You wake up at the crack of dawn. You point out "Quincy Marketplace" on the map for the fiftieth time. You repress the urge to say, "Please! Can't you read a guidebook?" It is only Day Four, but one glance in the mirror and you see puffy eyes, dirty jeans, and bedhead. What happened to you? You try to wipe the sleep from your eyes, but there's no time. You're already late for the 8 AM breakfast at the CHEERS bar.

If your in-laws are intent on staying on your pullout couch, there are pros and cons to opening your guest room versus booking them a suite at the Marriott.

> "My in-laws stayed in my apartment for 10 days. When I left for work, they began their work. They washed our dishes. They cleaned the crumbs INSIDE our toaster. They vacuumed pet beds and even ran vinegar in my humidifiers. I thought this was wonderful. I mean—it wasn't like I was asking them to do it. My husband got mad at me when I 'accidentally' left out my scuffed leather boots and the shoe polish. He thought I was taking it too far."
>
> LYNN, NEW YORK CITY

> "My fiancé and I opened our home to our in-laws. We didn't think it would be an issue. But after the third day of the weeklong trip, we felt crammed and stressed. We told them that a friend of ours was out of town and said we could stay at his place. We assured them that it wasn't a problem at all. What we didn't tell them is that we checked into

a hotel and luxuriated. It was like we were on vacation!"

JANETTE, CHICAGO

You and your sweetie must carve out time to be alone. This is easier if your in-laws are staying in a hotel, but you can always shut your bedroom door. When you hear "But my family is only here for two weeks!" remind him that alone time doesn't have to occupy an entire night. Take a post-dinner walk. Catch a movie or go to the gym together. Have sex in the guest room while your in-laws are busy watching "the good TV" in your bedroom. Whatever the event, you need to recharge.

In-law visits are not about putting your life on hold. If they are visiting you, that means they took vacation or early retirement. You have a job, a life, and a relationship to protect. If you don't call a time-out, you will crack and snap at your partner, his parents, and anyone who dares look in your direction, so help you Jesus. It won't be pretty.

After their stay, if your in-laws threaten to buy the house next door because "it's a great real estate opportunity," here are a few things you can do to deter them:

- Remind them how wonderful their life is where they live. Their friends will miss them. Max, their dachshund, doesn't like change. You suspect your mailman steals your Valu-Pak coupons.
- Prepare a horrible moving story. Your friend's mom moved to be closer to her grandkids, and the moving guys stole all of her belongings. When she filed a police report, they found her best china strewn across train tracks, linens on fire, and a note that said, "You shouldn't have."

- Make peace with empty promises to relocate closer to them. Remember when his mom promised to keep her wedding guest list to fifty people? This is the same thing. Fight fire with fire and lie: "No need for you to move. We'll relocate near you in two years. I promise!"

### A Full Tank of Gas Away

You visit on weekends, holidays, and hot summer days (they have a pool). Their house is your country home, medicine cabinet, and office supply depot. Chances are they're hyperaware of your social life and know when they're not invited to your dinner parties.

You can't believe how happy you were when the price of gas shot up. It did cut down on their drive-by visits. However, a few books-on-tape later and your in-laws are on the sidelines cheering at every race, triathlon, and cancer walk that you do. And they're there to celebrate your big day turning 30, 31, and 32!

This is a family that doesn't believe in "minor events." Otherwise, they wouldn't have anywhere to go. Driving the open road brings them to their purpose in life—you.

> "My sister-in-law lives three hours away. One time, I borrowed $300 from her. It's the never-ending saga of my life. I paid her back, but it's like blood money. She asks me to do things for her all the time. Please visit her sick friend. Come and pick out colors for the bathroom. It was like I owed her my kidney. At some point, I wished I did. Point of my story is don't borrow money from in-laws that live nearby. Borrow from a friend. You'll never live it down."
>
> SUSAN, ST. PAUL

So how can you sate your in-laws' travel bug, but keep them at arm's length when you really don't want visitors?

- **Jump in the car.** A preemptive jaunt to their town could get you off the hook for other occasions. If you take the initiative, you'd be surprised how much they'll appreciate your visit and quell their desperate need to check up on you.
- **Meet halfway.** A two-hour lunch at an equidistant Olive Garden counts as quality time, and you don't have to provide the Hospitaliano with a side of garlic bread.
- **Make a standing date.** This is particularly useful with extended in-law families living within a 50-mile radius. Each party can be responsible for a rotating family gathering. Between Mom and Dad and the three siblings, you'll host maybe three potlucks a year, and on the other dates, you control your arrival and departure times. Get out before your brother-in-law starts singing show tunes. Why does he do that?

## You Vote at the Same High School Gym

You shop at the same deli counter and eye the same low-fat tuna salad. On a romantic Friday night, you and your sweetie snuggle at a corner table in your favorite restaurant when dessert is delivered *on the house.* Then you discover your in-laws wildly waving from across the aisle.

There are no secrets when you live in the same zip code. Your in-law discovers the retirement community pamphlet you sent away for. Lying there on the counter, it ruins your in-law relationship, a good fifteen years ahead of schedule. "What is this? You're planning to lock me away?" your in-law demands. A tin of homemade cookies is thrown at you. That hurts.

> "I went to Home Depot with my husband and his mother after we decided to redo our bathroom. I walked down an aisle and found my mother-in-law sitting on a toilet, smiling: 'You never know exactly what the fit is going to be, until you sit on it. I like this one. I use your bathroom all the time, so my vote counts.'"
>
> JOANN, NEW ORLEANS

### Working with Your In-Laws

Maybe you're living in the same town as your in-law because you work together. Your slogan: "I'm now CEO of my grandfather-in-law's cement company—thanks, Pupup!"

Issues arise when you and your in-law share a work parking lot. Pay—is it equal among all in-laws? Do you have regular job reviews? Is there a written job description, or is it like everything else in the family . . . they assume you know the deal.

If you work at a company that employs both relatives and nonfamily employees, is it fair and balanced for both? There must be clear communication regarding "special compensation" arrangements regarding use of the company car, the company VIP box at the Lakers game, and the company Visa card. Remember those 1980s full-page ads for Aussie shampoo, with all the relatives poised in their bathrobes and shiny hair? Now you know that beneath those enviable tresses, someone was dying inside. With hope, it won't be you.

Every day your in-law swings open the back door saying: "Hiyeeeee!" No, this isn't a sitcom. This is your life. They know your golf schedule, that you just bought ankle-high black boots, and where to find Raymond, your hairstylist. It's easy to feel overwhelmed and intruded upon.

You *can* teach an old dog new tricks. It isn't easy, but with practice and incentive, your old dog will roll over. Here are a few sanity retention techniques for you:

- You're no Martha Stewart. There is never enough time to clean before your in-laws' every surprise appearance, so they find out quickly what unscooped kitty litter smells like. Dishes get washed when the sink is full, not before, and that's where your shoes *go*. If their comments about housekeeping persist, kindly take away their key.
- Give Mr. and Mrs. Determined-to-Be-in-Your-Life a mind-numbing project that soaks up their time but doesn't involve spending even more time with you. Need a new home stereo system? Let them do the legwork. Present it enthusiastically: "This will make a huge difference in our lives." Tell them it needs a video input so you can watch your father-in-law's home movies. And then drop them off at Circuit City.
- Limit forms of communication. Do you talk by phone? Or do they just stop by? In either case, set firm early-morning and late-night limits. You relish sleeping in on the weekends, so calls before 10 AM are not okay and will not be answered. Ditto for drop-bys after 10 PM. Say that you're "trying for a family." They'll back off, but still might root through your trash cans for the home pregnancy test results while you sleep.
- Don't blur the boundaries. When you run out of eggs,

don't be tempted to grab them from your in-laws' fridge. As soon as you do, you're inviting your in-laws to do the same. Get dressed and go to the store. Do unto others, and all that.

There is a silver lining to this dark cloud. Aside from the warmth and support of extended family, your in-laws help out when your 60-gallon fish tank leaks and you're in London. They've already met your landlord, Larry. They might get him to fix that light on the porch and clean the carpets, too, since they found out how much rent you pay for "that dump."

### You Share a Wireless Internet Connection

Every night you watch *Access Hollywood* with your new roommate, your younger sister-in-law. Sure, she's working a summer internship with the *San Francisco Chronicle,* which you support. But she just used the last of the skim milk, flooded the bathroom (the plastic layer goes *inside* the bathtub!), and invited her scantily clad college-age girlfriends to lounge on your couch. Naturally, she's wearing on your nerves.

Remember this: the in-law who lives with you is the in-law you can yell at. No longer do they get the fringe benefits of not being "a blood relative" and not "knowing you very well." Every single morning you'll find her in your bathrobe watching *Good Morning America* on your TV.

This living situation was supposed to be temporary. But so was the bridge on your bottom row of teeth. That's still around. So is your in-law. She has flourished in your apartment like a roach infestation, and you need to exterminate.

It's a slippery slope if you don't set boundaries. Don't be

afraid to be explicitly clear: "You know, we set aside the den for you. Please eat Lucky Charms in your space—the den—not my bed." Then toss her the multicolored pillow you embroidered with the phrase: "Absence Makes the Heart Grow Fonder."

Now, if your in-law had to flee home and community for sudden and terrible reasons, be hospitable. It's only a temporary inconvenience for you. It's a life-shattering situation for them. When your in-law leaves a hairbrush on the coffee table and relocates a church group to your kitchen, deal by venting to friends and having your partner handle the details pertaining to his family member. You shouldn't have to tell your father-in-law that pants are required clothing for dinner.

> "When my mother-in-law had to quickly flee her home because of massive flooding, she only had time to grab the most important things to her. In addition to photo albums and family jewelry, she grabbed some of the athletic shrine of her son's glory days twelve years ago. Isn't that ridiculous?"
>
> NICOLE, BATON ROUGE

Is there an added benefit to the roommate in-law? Sure! If you're stranded in a snowstorm, blizzard, or airport, and you *must* check your e-mail and stock quotes, you can call home and have your in-law do it. You'll just have to ignore the snarky comments about your e-mail password and lagging portfolio performance.

Of course, an in-law living with you can also be an in-law that pitches in to help. Your brother-in-law is a fantastic chef (who knew lemongrass and tofu tasted that good?) and a wonderful babysitter. It's not always a terrible thing that he's joined your brood.

Here's how to balance the desire to be hospitable and the responsibilities of a visiting in-law:

**For one week:** Wait on them, tend to their every whim. This means stocking the fridge with Coors Light, organizing poker night at your place, and marinating the buffalo wings two days before in-law arrival.

**After one week:** You cook; they clean. Or vice versa. You get TV dibs at night; they get to watch your ESPN all day long. If they offer to stick around for hours to wait for the plumber, you'll gladly furnish an updated version of the Sims video game to keep them busy.

**After two weeks:** It's time for the housebound in-law to go on laundry duty—BUT—you'll take their dress shirts and sweaters to the dry cleaner on your way to work. You need a night out alone; have them babysit or dog walk this Friday. They need the car on Saturday? No problem! You've got some sleeping in to do—you'll even spring for gas.

**After three weeks:** Time for your in-law to step up to the plate—literally. It's time your guest room, towels, wireless connection, and expensive bath products were offset by a nice dinner out. Hope they offer; if not, leave a bookmarked *Zagat's* under their pillow.

**One month plus:** Your in-law ought to be paying rent. Sheesh. In lieu of cold hard cash exchanging hands, your in-law should be offering to cook, clean, babysit, weed the garden, paint the fence, and participate in your neighborhood watch program. If after months of squatting—whether planned or sudden—your in-law hasn't settled into a reciprocal generosity routine, it's time for the sit-down. This is where your "better half" does the talking.

No matter where your in-laws live, you should have a secret code word with your partner—a sound (bird chirp), a word (sonar), or a dance number (the Worm) that advertises the end of the visit. If your in-law yammers in your living room and you can't take it anymore, bust it out. For example: "Hon, I just ordered a transducer for my sonar machine." Now you both know it's time to drive your in-law to the Holiday Inn or escort her to the air mattress in the dining room.

## Blue States vs. Red States

There are culture clashes. This is glaringly obvious on Election Day, and it's something you noted the minute you inherited in-laws.

Thank you, Jet Blue. More flight offerings at reasonable prices means more in-laws in the air. When your in-laws step foot in your home, they bring a little something from whence they came. It's like when the Spaniards brought influenza to the Native Americans, and we know how that turned out.

Where on the map your in-laws live helps define their "regionalized personality." Are they southerners who panic when forced to drive in the snow? Are they midwesterners who chat for hours with "nice telemarketers"? Or are they high-strung New Yorkers who snap at coffee baristas who can't multitask with the skim milk—precious seconds are being wasted! Pour it FASTER and stop talking!! Whatever the geographical influence, you can anticipate certain behaviors.

Stuff this map in your wallet or car sun visor. It will help you. After all, a little respect for what they call "home" might illuminate why they sleep with a harpoon under their pillow. I said "might."

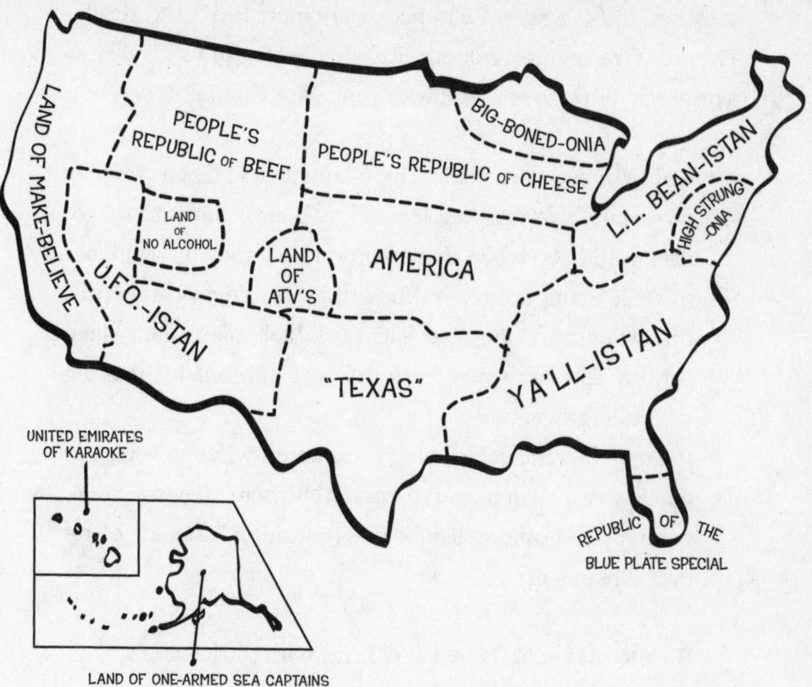


## Regional Guide to In-Laws

There are seven territories of in-law personalities in this great country of ours. Each has its own unique flavor.

### 1. West Coast In-Laws (California, Oregon, Washington)

Three words: Burning Man Festival. Your in-laws live where Manifest Destiny carried them. They come from a long line of gold hunters—those in search of a truer, richer way of life. Every single Napa Valley wine they uncork, or Starbucks coffee they brew, or macrobiotic muffin they bake, they judge you for not living the way they do. "Oh, West Coast people are more laid back." Really? They're ultra-aggressive about lifestyle choices and the 40-hour workweek! How do you deal with your West Coast in-laws?

- Compliment their tan. Their sunglasses. Their shapely mountain-bike sculpted legs. They'll eat it up (those egotists!). And coo when they mention how they fly seaplanes to their island house, and how the orca whales and "pristine wilderness" are their backyard. Blah, blah, blah. Make sure to note how very fresh the air is, even if it's making your allergies act up.
- Read up on renewable energy resources: wind power, solar energy, and corn-powered cars. Tell them that you're already on the waiting list for one (a waiting list made of recycled paper, no less).

**How to dress:** In flannel and Tevas with thick socks.
**What not to do:** Smoke cigarettes. Joints, however, are cool.

## 2. Rocky Mountain In-Laws (Colorado, Montana, Idaho, Utah)

Your rugged in-laws know a thing or two about machinery. They can plow. They can drive a tractor. They can dig a deep hole with a backhoe (and I'm talking about Aunt Trudy on dialysis here). They can also wrangle sheep on a mountain without the help of a gay lover (no matter what that movie said). How do you impress in-laws that live in winter for nine months a year and are known to wrestle bears for sport?

- If your weenie job as an economics professor hasn't prepared you for life with these in-laws, buying a picture book about tractors and trucks—something a five-year-old boy would drool over—will help. At least you'll know your trenchers from your dozers and your grapple log skidders from your pipe layers.

- Pick an alpine sport: ice climbing, fly-fishing, kayaking, mountain climbing, trekking, snowshoeing, skiing, or mountain biking, and excel at it. It doesn't matter if you live in Florida, you need to train so you can join your in-laws in death-defying "leisure sports" at high altitude (with no bleeping oxygen!).

**How to dress:** In jeans and a warm jacket, because you'll be outside shoveling hay.

**What not to do:** Mention how your gay brother in Boston just got married and a drag queen performed the ceremony.

### 3. Southwestern In-Laws (New Mexico, Arizona, Nevada)

There are two kinds of ex-hippie in-laws in the Southwest: those with boatloads of money and those with a jar of pennies. Figure out which one your in-law is. The former has a perfect golf swing, and the latter reliably has peyote.

When your Southwest in-laws hug you, they practically blind—the sun glints off their turquoise jewelry and belt buckles, sending signals miles into the sky. (Duh, that's how the aliens found Roswell.)

Your in-laws are into spirituality with a capital *S*. Every inch of wall space is covered with pottery depictions of Kokopelli and watercolor drawings of pueblos and adobe homes in rust and muted orange hues. They subsist on roasted green chilies and yerba mate. They also don't age. Is it the desert? The dry heat? Each time you see them, they're younger. In fact, they're twenty-five years old right now. It's terrifying.

How do you ingratiate yourself with southwestern in-laws?

- Go hot-air ballooning with your in-laws! Everyone in the Southwest does it. How else do you pass the time in 100-degree heat? Remember, hot-air balloons aren't just for Dorothy & Co. They're for you, your in-laws, and nineteenth-century explorers.
- Vegas, baby! Anyone? Slot machines? Showgirls? People-watching? Shark tank at Mandalay Bay? (These are rhetorical questions. You don't have to answer them.) But you may want to propose them to your in-laws, when they bust out the tarot cards—again. Hey, why don't you use those tarot cards to predict some winning hands of blackjack? As they say in the movies, it's just crazy enough to work, boss.

**How to dress:** A brightly patterned sundress and a necklace made of the largest beads known to man.

**What not to do:** Say you prefer modern art.

## 4. Texan In-Laws

Your Texan in-laws are smug about one thing: being Texan. We know you were once a republic! And everything's bigger! Six flags, the Alamo, that 72-ounce steak, and especially the hats. Fine! Texas is big, "American," flashy, *and* the center of the world.

If your Texan in-laws aren't gorgeously well-manicured people from Houston or Dallas, or cultured Austinites, they're ranchers and they don't give a damn about you, "the en-vi-ro-mentalists," and "the gov'nment." After all, the rest of the world is just not Texas.

Of course, you'll meet a second cousin-in-law that uses her panty hose to strain motor oil, but the rest of the family isn't too proud of her. So how do you deal with the Texan in-laws?

- Accept that a lot of people you'll meet in the Lone Star State will have nicknames like Joe-Bob, Billy-Bob, Jim-Bob, Little John, Big John, etc. You'll be expected to know about their souped-up truck and new gun rack in intimate detail.
- Respect the laws of the Barcalounger. Your Texan in-laws don't have normal chairs; they need something with a footrest. Succumb to the relaxation factor of holding conversations while horizontal.

**How to dress:** A "Don't Mess with Texas" T-shirt with a Stetson hat, only because your in-laws gave them to you upon your arrival.

**What not to do:** Forget to send good wishes to your in-laws on Texan holidays like Texas Independence Day, the start of Deer Hunting Season, the Opening Day of high school football practice, and the day the new model year of Ford F-150s hits the market.

## 5. Southern In-Laws

### (Arkansas, Louisiana to Florida, and up to Kentucky and Virginia)

Your in-laws love NASCAR. If they don't, their neighbors do. Your southern in-laws are either "refined city folk" or "simple country folk," and they'll want you to know the difference.

Your southern in-laws are suspicious of you. It's not just you—it's anyone outside their state. Your in-laws have never been "North," and by that, they mean Delaware. It's not that they don't want to go, just why would they? People have been in their town for generations. It's home, which is why you should move there. When you're south of the Mason-Dixon Line, do as those who live south of the Mason-Dixon Line . . .

- Learn the key players in "the Confederacy." How many times have you met a southerner named Jefferson Davis? Billions? Every street, building, and public school is named after these folks: Stonewall Jackson, Robert E. Lee, Jeb Stuart, Alexander Stephens, P. T. Beauregard, or Nathan Bedford Forrest. But please never, ever mention the Destroyer-of-the-South, Yankee General Sherman. He's still on their "list," 150 years later.
- Talk the talk. Know southern sport rivalries and which side you're on with the Tar Heels vs. Blue Devils, LSU vs. Ole Miss, and Tennessee Volunteers vs. Kentucky Wildcats.

**How to dress:** Something bright and feminine from your mother's closet.

**What not to do:** Don't call it the "Civil War." It's the "War of Northern Aggression."

### 6. Northeast Corridor In-Laws (Ohio, Pennsylvania, and up through Maine)

If you or anyone you're related to went to a fancy school, now's the time to mention it. New Englanders love to think "they know better" and that "they are smarter" and that they "vote correctly." They can push up their dark-framed glasses and snub you with their "Plymouth Rock" crap.

The crowded cities and suburbs of Philadelphia, Washington, D.C., Cincinnati, New York, and Boston mean one thing—your in-laws *are* the diversity in America. They smother you with affection because a hundred other relatives live down the street.

- Join the rat race. You must keep up with the Joneses—the family that you can see from the bay window in your in-laws' kitchen. Last week, the competition was about the house gutters. They won. This week it's about you. Who has the sweetest daughter-in-law?
- Your northern in-laws have summer homes in non-warm places like Nantucket. What's the point?

**How to dress:** Like you just fell out of the J. Crew catalog.

**What not to do:** Mention that you didn't vote in the last election.

### 7. Midwestern In-Laws (Indiana to Missouri, up to North Dakota and Michigan)

If a giant, two-headed reptilian monster was heading toward your in-laws' subdivision, they would smile and wave. Your in-laws are *that* friendly and nice. Sometimes it's creepy. Like the time they offered a teenager a ride back to his college campus—it looked an awful lot like kidnapping.

Between the ice fishing, apple-pie baking, and dining at Perkins Restaurant and Bakery (which they nicknamed Pukins), your big-boned in-laws spend a lot of time driving (8 hours is short haul), using terms like "who gives a flying fig," and asking "how ya doing?" followed by "okey, dokey!" So how do you get ahead with them?

- Dig into dishes that involve massive amounts of melted cheese. Your in-laws will prepare cheesy potatoes, cheesy broccoli, cheesy asparagus, and fried cheese curds—which sounds awful, but c'mon, let's admit it, a little melted cheese makes everything better.
- "Live simply, so that others can simply live." If your in-laws aren't city dwellers, they're farmers and they know how to birth a cow, mend a horse, or feed a pig. If you know zilch about farms, don't fret. Praise the good bugs—ladybugs, lacewings, hoverflies, and honeybees—and chastise the potentially bad bugs—flea hoppers, lygus bugs, aphids, and mealy bugs. Impress your in-laws by differentiating good stinkbugs (they're green) from bad ones (they're brown).

**How to dress:** Something with an elastic waistband.
**What not to do:** Take shortcuts. Using life's conveniences (leaf blower vs. rake, microwave vs. Crock-Pot, etc.) only means you're not working hard enough!

## Breathing "Om"

Regardless of how far your in-laws traveled and from where, try to infuse tranquility in your home. Feng shui practice advises making an offering to the northeast corner of your home, which is your family sector. In this area, place a potted plant, dangle a crystal, or hang a harmonious photo.

This doesn't mean a poster of an eagle soaring above a mountain range with the word *S-U-C-C-E-S-S*. Nope. That's a print you'd find in a high school guidance counselor's office. Find an image that truly speaks to you and makes you feel peaceful.

Making an effort to focus on improving the family area of your life may ease your next in-law visit. Or it may cause you to hurl your mother-in-law's suppositories into the expensive water fountain you bought. Why do you keep finding them in the couch cushions?

Just remember, now they're on your turf. In a few short months, it will be the holidays and you might be a houseguest in their home. *Sigh*.

# the holiday scramble

## Short tempers, dirty dishes, and the pullout couch

EXCERPT FROM THE AUTHOR'S DIARY:

> *My father-in-law tried to feed me freshly carved turkey directly from his hand. I think we're entering new and uncomfortable territory. While I appreciate the gesture and implied closeness, it made me feel like the family poodle. Must discuss with husband.*

### The Most Wonderful Time of the Year

Season's Greetings! Whatever signals the beginning of your holiday celebration—hanging red lanterns, completing a month-long fast, or squealing as the SpongeBob SquarePants float makes his way down Broadway—it's a jolly time of the year.

Blinking lights strangle the office cooler. Neighbors gift-wrap their front doors. Megawatt nativity scenes confuse the wildlife. Your sense of normalcy and restraint is tossed out the faux-frosted window, when:

- You trade your velvet skirt for blue and gold felt Hanukah pants.
- Your usual "Hello, neighbor" is replaced with "*Habari, gani?*" for Kwanzaa.
- You morph into a 5-day part-ay machine for Diwali! Who wants Jell-O shots? They're for Lakshmi—the goddess of light!
- You become a beast at the Eid el-Fitr feast after Ramadan. How many *sambousehs* can you fit in your mouth at one time? Six? Seven?

Whether it's Oshugatsu (Japanese New Year), Bodhi Day (celebration of Shakyamuni Buddha), or Día de Los Reyes (Spanish/ Latin celebration of Three Kings Day), days blur into a joyous haze, and on a Tuesday morning, you awaken and ask: What happened? Where am I?

Still, despite the holiday chaos, this is the time of year when you focus on charity—giving to your postman, giving to the Will Smith Foundation, and, of course, giving to your in-laws.

> "I'm hoping to use the last of my vacation days . . . (inhale) . . . to spend the holidays with my in-laws. Yes, we're driving this year. No, they don't have cable. Yes, it's seven hours away. Without traffic."
>
> You, this year

We've all had to tell our friends and coworkers about our holiday vacations with in-laws and we try to sound upbeat. You tell yourself, "*Oh, it won't be that bad.*" You dream of color-coordinating pantsuits with your sister-in-law. You envision high-fiving your father-in-law for his phenomenal Scattergories performance. You imagine giggling with your boyfriend's nana while watching her favorite *Golden Girls* episode where Blanche gets tested for STDs.

Norman Rockwell would be proud, but we all know that Norman was likely on some heavy mood-altering drugs. Short of hitting up his secret stash, here's some advice to make the holidays hassle-free.

### His Parents' Place or Yours?

His house is cramped with hundreds of little cousins running around, and your place has spiders, a loud TV, and a pullout couch to sleep on. So, how does a young couple choose which family to celebrate with? Start by asking yourself: what are you looking for? If the answer is *a couple's weekend in St. Barts*, that's impossible—unless of course your in-laws live there, and if they do, then you're the luckiest girl in the world and this author hates you and all your duty-free perfumes.

But seriously, do you want to watch PBS every night in Maine or head into downtown Pittsburgh for a night of binge drinking? Either way, there are pros and cons to each home. Inevitably, your in-laws have a working CD player while your family still plays Joan Baez's holiday tunes on an 8-track. But when it comes down to it, you must choose to celebrate in a single nuthouse. Don't worry—in a few short months you'll rotate nuthouses for the next holiday.

#### ♥ ♥ ♥ ♥ ♥ 10 REASONS WHY ♥ ♥ ♥ ♥ ♥

**YOUR PARENTS PLACE IS PERFECT FOR THE HOLIDAYS**

1. Tammy, your high school friend, still lives at home and dates a townie bartender = free beers.

2. Purple gymnastic awards blanket your walls. Your flexibility is legendary.
3. There are no "mystery meat" casseroles on your dinner table, only Frosted Flakes.
4. You feel dressed up in flannel pajama bottoms and Hard Rock Cafe sweatshirt.
5. Your parents don't perpetuate the Santa myth. You are allowed to get up and pee in the middle of the night without disturbing "the elves."
6. Your own dog won't growl at you, sniff out your bra, and carry it into the TV room.
7. You're free to leave the house without a trail of bread crumbs behind you.
8. It isn't considered rude when your grandmother tells you about her GI woes, dental implants, and recent discovery of the benefits of green tea, and you just nod, "That's great, Grandma," and continue to read the paper.
9. You're allowed to turn down the volume of Meshuge Klezmer's "Dreidel Song."
10. You can answer the house phone without being asked, "Who is this? Where's Janet? Is this the housekeeper? Are you supposed to be answering the phone?"

## ♥ ♥ ♥ ♥ ♥ 10 REASONS WHY ♥ ♥ ♥ ♥ ♥

### HIS PARENTS PLACE IS PERFECT FOR THE HOLIDAYS

1. When his Aunt Emily comments on your blemish, she also offers a gratis treatment for your crow's-feet with the dermatologist she keeps on retainer.
2. His family won't beg you to do your Jay Leno impression.

3. You'll learn a lot from N'Gwesi, their exchange student, just in time for your grad school term paper on "Irrigation Systems in Third World Nations."
4. The group spinning class they signed everyone up for will help you work off that second helping of pie.
5. The hot water in his house never fades mid-exfoliation.
6. You can study his prom photos.
7. You can meet his high school friends and cross-reference with his prom photos.
8. The dinner conversation centers on property taxes, not the time you got caught playing "doctor" with the neighbor boy when you were five years old.
9. Your in-laws have digital cable, DVR, *and* a working remote.
10. You get to sleep in the same room.

## The Holiday Auction Block

> "Let's see, in 1999 we spent Christmas with my family, New Year's with his, and then my parents made that surprise trip in February, so we felt obligated to visit my in-laws at Easter even though they live six hours away and aren't Christian. Now wait, who gets Earth Day again? And did my mother-in-law really call 'dibs' on Columbus Day weekend 2012?"
>
> YOU, AGAIN THIS YEAR

Spending time with your family is always a "treat," but for holidays it's pretty much a requirement. With a new family in the mix, you become lady justice. You have the new responsibility to keep things fair and balanced in your courtroom. (But be nice about it—you're not Judge Judy.) Here are some ways to avoid letting pressure, guilt, and manipulation from one family ruin a lovely week with the other side.

### Problem Scenario: Everyone Wants You for Christmas

Some holidays are in high demand. Others lack the "it" factor. Nobody cares if you celebrate Election Day by yourself in a bathrobe, eating dried soups out of a chipped mug.

> **Solution:** Balance popular holidays by rotating on an every-other-year schedule between families. Make this plan known to all involved, and request up front that they respect your Solomon-like attempts to split your time equally. If Granny Mee-maw is making your favorite chocolate pecan pie THIS YEAR AND THIS YEAR ONLY!, it's called FedEx, if she really wants to treat you.

### Problem Scenario: Hungry, Hungry In-Laws (for Your Vacation Days)

To join your in-laws for a weeklong Alaskan cruise in July, you used five vacation days. Thank you—the whale watching was splendid and the one-armed sea captains surprisingly friendly. Technically, you also "owe" your in-laws this year's Thanksgiving, but the long weekend your boss offered is also the only time you can spare to see your own parents.

> **Solution:** You choose your family. Why? Because you had quality time with your in-laws recently, and you withdrew from the vacation-day bank to do so. There's no overdraft protection, and your folks deserve an interest payment now and again. Hey, sitting opposite your own Uncle Frank at the dinner table has lots in common with whale watching, so it's only fair.

### Problem Scenario: Your Family Loves Groundhog Day!

Some holidays are really important to one family and completely irrelevant to another.

> **Solution:** Announce that you'll attend the Groundhog Day brunch with your family, since your mother-in-law can't even pronounce "Punxsutawney Phil." Similarly, if your father-in-law is Greek and March 25, Greek Independence Day, is his favorite day of the year, make the trip, and set aside time for a nice, long phone call with your own dad. Who are you kidding? Your dad doesn't talk on the phone! Easy.

### Problem Scenario: A Sick Relative

A close family member is ill and can't travel in the foreseeable future.

> **Solution:** Damn those laws of physics! You just can't be in two places at once. This is one of those times when you and your sweetie might want to fly solo and spend time alone with each of your families. Or begin the holiday apart and reconvene after your individual obligations have been met. Things can change in a year, so even if you spent last Christmas with your folks, maybe this is one tree trimming you shouldn't miss. Most in-law families respect this kind of decision making, but if they complain or put pressure on you, tell them that if the tables were turned, you would do the same for them and empty their bed pan.

### Problem Scenario: A Family Event Coincides with a Holiday

Your brother's thirtieth birthday bash is on St. Patrick's Day—a holiday you normally spend with your enthusiastically Irish in-laws.

**Solution:** As soon as you know about the party, alert your in-laws—well in advance. Then offer an intermittent holiday as payback. Maybe a surprise Mother's Day visit? They only live 3 hours away by car, and you'll surely win extra points for your thoughtfulness. (Unfortunately, these points are not redeemable at Victoria's Secret.)

There, now you're juggling two families like Tom Jones juggles panties at the MGM Grand. You know where you're heading for most holidays, you have preplanned excuses for the others, and a few wild cards in reserve. Relax! Dye some Easter eggs, light a sparkler, and hang a wreath while convincing your in-laws that going to a restaurant for Thanksgiving is easier for everybody. You're a pro. That is, until you remember your sweetie has a stepfamily. Oh right, those people.

## The Stepfamily Code

What if it's not just two families you're splitting holiday time with, but three . . . or four? Now, the holidays snowball into buying gifts for people you barely ever see and flying across the Great Plains to accommodate step-siblings who have in-law commitments of their own. Here are tips for coexisting peacefully with large mixed families during the most wonderful—and stressful—times of the year:

- **Tap the others of your generation to plan a holiday strategy.** You and your stepsister-in-law don't want to travel five hours to the family picnic. She'd rather spend Labor Day cleaning and readying her kids for kindergarten. Together, focus on your in-laws' Maui time-share. Bingo!

- **Take the initiative and reorient the family gathering.** Instead of the family picnic, plan this year's Hanukah in Maui, Hawaii-style: Pineapple latkes! Ukulele hora songs! And just maybe your in-laws will kick in for airfare. Thank you, frequent flier miles.
- **"Excuses, excuses."** Don't wait for your stepmother-in-law to ask you face-to-face what your plans are for June 14. Without a solid reason, it's impossible to turn down her Flag Day potluck. Just say: "We can't make plans until I know my work schedule. I'll keep you posted!" Or: "We don't know our weekend plans yet, since we entered a time-share in Napa Valley." A rehearsed excuse is the best excuse, even if it's fake. (We know you can't afford a time-share in Napa. But good one!)
- **The preemptive strike.** You know what's going to happen when you tell your mother-in-law you're spending Thanksgiving with her ex-husband and his child bride. She's going to grit her teeth and ask if you can spend Christmas with her, fully knowing this year it's with your folks.

    If you take ten minutes to map this conversation in your mind, you'll realize what she *really* wants is for you to attend her birthday party. But she'll never say it. Here's a clever predetermined reply, brought to you by Mistress Subliminal:

> You know what, Marge? We're bummed to miss you over Thanksgiving (you passive-aggressive killjoy). What about a quick trip to your place (den of horrors) for your birthday? I'd love to give you a hand with the party arrangements (I'd rather stick a spoon in my eye). Sound good?

However, if you know you're already booked for her birthday, skip to the next happy occasion you'll be sharing together. It eases the disappointment. Here's another possible response, from the Mistress Subliminal archives:

> Marge, we'd love to spend Thanksgiving with you and attend your birthday party (if we were blasted out of our minds), but we're saving our vacation days for your niece's upcoming wedding (and for the Daytona 500). You wanted us there all week, right? (Needy.) We just bought the tickets yesterday. (Still need to do that.) We're so excited!

### How Much Do I Love Thee, Stepfamily?

With the natural tug-of-war that stepfamilies and holidays create, it's hard not to resent extra family members. To keep your cool, identify what's really important:

- How close is your sweetie to his stepparent? If the answer is "Not Close," then crossing twelve states to celebrate Easter is absurd. Please, reassess.
- What if your partner adores his half siblings, but isn't close with his stepparent? Instead of making the trek to their place in Nova Scotia, invite your half brother to visit you for a long weekend. You'll see all those other people at the next wedding—that's what weddings are for!

Of course, your boss doesn't understand that you have four sets of family to visit, and that your 12 vacation days aren't enough. Nobody cares—especially not HR. So sometimes your partner should go it alone. You simply can't keep up with the number of times his family falls in love, remarries, births children, and then divorces. There are only 365 days a year.

Now that you've divvied up your calendar, you realize: Sometimes you win, and sometimes the house wins. But somewhere in between lie the overlooked, bonus rounds of holiday betting. Make sure you don't miss these gems . . .

### Why Dating a Jewish Guy at Christmas Rocks!

The interfaith union is really at its strongest this time of year because you don't have to choose anything. It's Christmas with your family *forever*. It's simple, for once.

"December 25 is a day you don't want to run out of shaving cream. Except for the local Hunan Wok and Ming Palace, everything shuts down. Now, as a Jew on Christmas, I can't fill my prescriptions, but I can chow down on fruitcake with my in-laws, while watching *Julio Iglesias Live,* on the TV—you know the one where he sings from some cathedral in Spain? Not too shabby!"

LARRY, LOS ANGELES

### You're Not Christian: Why Dating One at Christmas Rocks!

You've never tasted spiked egg nog. You thought "mistletoe" was a medical condition. Well, now's your chance to don a white beard, slide down chimneys, and tie green and red ribbon around everything, especially pets. Finally, you're on the inside. So, wake up on December 25 and rejoice in rampant consumerism! Go ahead! You deserve it.

"I'm Hindu and I've only celebrated Christmas with a few friends growing up. Now my boyfriend, an Episcopalian, invites me to his family's house for the holidays. I never understood cutting a tree and killing it to bring it inside. I'm not saying I support it, but it is very pretty!"

BRINDA, NEW ORLEANS

## The Trojan Horse: Gifts and How to Interpret Their Hidden Meaning

"Oh, what a pretty bow!" you exclaim. This little pink present can be a Pandora's box of insecurity and resentment. Sometimes, what seems like a sweet gift is actually one that says your SAT score brings down the family average.

> "Getting gifts from my in-laws is like being on *Extreme Makeover*. Last Christmas, I was given Proactiv, the acne medicine. This Christmas, my mother-in-law told me her gift will change my skin from Nicole Kidman–pale to Jennifer Lopez–gold. The present was self-tanning cream. The card read: 'To Joanna, for your health.'"
>
> JOANNA, CHARLESTON

> "My in-laws recently returned from a life-altering trip to India. For Christmas, they gave me wooden bracelets, silk scarves, and a fertility statue."
>
> MELANIE, NEW HAVEN

It can be *so* confusing. You were almost certain they liked you, until you opened a tub of peach-scented hand cream—a gift that says, "I don't know you and I would give this to the nice lady at church whose name escapes me." Rest assured, most gifts are given with the best of intentions and purest of heart. But when questions arise and nagging doubt rears its ugly head, refer to this handy chart of common holiday gifts and how to interpret their hidden meaning.

**How to Interpret In-Law Gifts**

| The Gift | What They Say | What They Don't Say |
|---|---|---|
| J. Crew sweater | "I didn't know what size you were." | "I grabbed the largest size, Ms. Fatty McFat." |
| Subscription to *Parenting* | "Where are my grandkids?" | "Don't screw up my grandkids!" |
| 16" silver and sapphire necklace | "I really hope you like it!" | "It's not an engagement ring, but please stay with my son—the shmuck!" |
| Knitted cap | "I thought this color would look wonderful on you." | "We didn't know you were coming and found this upstairs." |
| *Jingle All the Way, Home Alone 2,* and *Christmas with the Kranks* DVDs | "It's *so* nice to finally meet you! My son hides all his girlfriends from me. I don't know why." | "I hope she likes the batteries, paper towels, oranges, and blank CDs I also got her from Costco." |
| Cotton dress from 1952 | "It's vintage." | "I've been meaning to clean out my closet." |
| Mug, wall calendar, or mousepad with family photo | "Just a little something silly from us to you." | "Think of us every morning. And then call us. If we don't call you first." |
| $100 check | "We know you don't need this." | "We know you need this." |
| Kitten calendar | "We know how much you and Dan adore cats." | "Where are my grandkids?!" |
| *Harrius Potter et Philosophi Lapis* (*Harry Potter* in Latin) | "We know it's not *The Real World, Vol. 7* DVD that you wanted . . ." | "But it will broaden your current vocabulary of 'totally,' 'like,' and 'cool.'" |
| "Live Strong" bracelet, tree in Israel, or a barrette made by tsunami victims | "Our family prioritizes giving our hearts to those less fortunate." | "Clearly, our son feels the same way." |
| Homemade ashtray | "I made it in my art class." | "I made it in my AA meeting." |
| Flannel pajama onesie | "Something cozy to put on after a long workday." | "It's a body condom." |

### A Shaving Kit? For *Me*?

No, it wasn't a mistake. Your gift was obviously intended for their son. Many daughters-in-law have been given a yarmulke, a massage appointment for (his) bad back, or a book about "business school grads and the road less traveled," overlooking the fact that you are a dancer. Smile. It's funny. Next year, tell them you want the jock strap in fuchsia. But if they continue to give you golf tee cuff links, start giving them gifts that are intended for you. It's only fair.

Fight passive-aggression with passive-aggression. Have your sweetie suggest a few gift-giving ideas to his family—gifts that seem like they're for him, but can be enjoyed by both of you. What about a $75 gift certificate to Smokey Bones Barbeque & Grill? Or whispering the words "theater tickets" into their ears? Your in-laws could even plan to join you. They get to spend more time with their son, while you sing along to songs from *Mamma Mia!*

### The Art of Re-Gifting

When your in-laws give you a "Sounds of the Sea" alarm clock, you can't immediately list it on eBay along with the used mattress pad you've been trying to unload. This gift is a talisman of guilt implanted in your home. When your in-laws visit, they want to see it. When they call, they want to hear it. So when they visit, plug it in the guest bedroom. Now the sounds of rolling surf and chirping seagulls will make *them* dream of sharks and missing surfer limbs. What goes around, comes around.

Gifts such as clothing, however, offer an excellent opportunity to exchange. "Oh shucks! The Cincinnati Bengals warm-up suit and matching socks are in the wash, *again*. But hey, check out the new sports watch I just got!" If you *must* re-gift, here are four words to live by: Little nieces love re-gifts. Finally, breathe a sigh of relief when you pawn George W. Bush's autobiography off on a five-year-old. She can use it as a drum kit along with those commemorative Gettysburg spoons your in-laws gave you last year.

Also, you can rid yourself of an undesired gift by telling your in-laws that you loved it so much you brought it to your office. This works with all decorative items—clocks, calendars, snow globes, etc. What are the chances your in-laws will ever see your office? They don't even know what you do for a living!

It's not just gifts that need interpretation; your in-laws need translation, too. Moments before the front door opens, you quickly run through your German in-laws' names again: Olaf, Brunhilde, Gretta . . . that's when you're warmly greeted, smothered with kisses, and hugged so tightly you can't breathe. But what does "*die ankunft*" mean?

## You Speak English. Unfortunately, No One Else Does

In the kitchen, your brother-in-law Giuseppe giggles and your father-in-law roars in laughter. In Italian, they have a moment. Your mother-in-law walks in carrying a plate, and they repeat the joke. She laughs so hard she's almost incontinent. Great-aunt Tina cackles from her wheelchair in the other room. It seems like a translation is near but the moment is lost when three cousins join the commotion. You pour yourself a glass of Chianti and curse your decision to buy *Music from* Grey's Anatomy—*Mix 4* instead of *Conversational Italian on Tape*.

It seems nowadays, most families speak English, just not your in-laws and not when you're around. "*Careculo!*" they yell, and you think: Are my in-laws referring to me? Or are they talking about their rotten neighbor's inability to collect the recycling bin? Maybe they're frustrated by the weather. It's hard to tell. Only later do you learn it's Spanish for "ass-face."

Be honest, you're in a dark cave of cultural despair this holiday season. Just assume they are saying:

- "Another girl who doesn't speak Mandarin!"
- "She's so tall and *so* white."
- "Honey? [yelling from another room] Do you still have the phone number of that dating service we got from your brother?"
- "She eats like a horse."

Because when you accept the worst, it's really not *that* bad. The most disconcerting thing isn't what they say, it's when you sit down with the family to play Scrabble and they bust out the Portuguese version. You couldn't feel more alone.

Clearly, there are thousands of different cultures in the world, but here are some insights from six women that will help you become as culturally smooth as Kofi Annan.

### Indian In-Laws . . . *according to Rashmi, Atlanta*

**TRUTHS:**

"Indian dancing, no matter what your boyfriend says, *is not just like hip hop.*"

**BEHAVIORS FROM THE OLD COUNTRY:**

"Grandparents burp. It's okay."

**THINGS PECULIAR TO HIS FAMILY, BUT MAY NOT BE CULTURAL:**

"My grandfather-in-law reads aloud every single road sign we drive past to practice his English. *Stop. Lotto $103 million jackpot. Twenty-seven miles to the freshest apples at Misconsett Farms.*"

**YOUR WINNING MOVE:**

"Remove your white high-tops when entering the house."

## Chinese In-Laws . . . *according to Lynn, San Francisco*

**YOUR "SPEAK AND SPELL" MOMENT:**

"You will recite in broken Mandarin: '*Ma ma ma ma?*' Translation: 'Did Mom scold the horse?' Oh, how they will laugh and laugh. Because of your poor inflection, you called his mom a horse. It's cool. You tried."

**WHERE ARE YOU SITTING?**

"At the place setting with the fork."

**KEEP YOUR PANTS ON, MS. TWO BEERS:**

"If you finish your beer or wine, relatives will keep pouring and toasting. It's best to take small sips. Also, wait to eat. Generally, the elders eat first and eventually they will invite you to dig in."

**YOUR WINNING MOVE WITH HIS MOM:**

"Compliment her cooking. She will insist that one dish is not cooked perfectly—too salty, not salty enough, overdone. It's simply a way for her to be humble. Do not agree with her. Whatever you do, don't give cooking advice. You're no Iron Chef."

## Trinidadian In-Laws . . . *according to Doris, New York*

**TRUTHS:**

"Homes are decorated with vibrant earth tones and filled with lots of tropical flowers. Typical meals include *callaloo* (spinach, okra, crabs, etc.) and *peleau* (meat, peas, pumpkin, rice)."

**YOUR GRANDFATHER-IN-LAW WILL:**

"Speak in patois. Expect to hear: '*Are you mamaguyan me?*' Which means: 'Are you fooling me?' "

**YOUR WINNING MOVE:**

"Spend an entire Saturday afternoon with his family barbecuing, leisurely enjoying yourself, with *no* plans to go anywhere else."

**HOW TO BLOW IT FOREVER:**

"Cheer for Barbados in cricket. Or support England in soccer. No drooling over David Beckham in their house!"

### Persian In-Laws . . . *according to Laleh, Bel-Air*

**TRUTHS:**

"Be ready for some *kookoo*. It's a saffron-spiced Iranian New Year's dish. And whether you're a Farsi-speaking grandmother or a six-year-old boy, everyone knows what a Pepsi is. It's a good icebreaker."

**WHEN FARSI DOESN'T TRANSLATE WELL INTO ENGLISH:**

"The word for popcorn in Farsi literally translates to *elephant farts*."

**HOW TO BLOW IT FOREVER:**

"In the bathroom, you may find a pitcher beside the toilet. It's not a watering can and please do not offer to refresh the plants with it."

**WHO YOU SHOULD NAME-DROP:**

"Andre Agassi, of course! He's half-Persian."

**YOUR WINNING MOVE:**

"Be the fun-loving multitasking houseguest: drink tea and play backgammon."

## Colombian In-Laws . . . *according to Erica, Los Angeles*

**TRUTHS:**

"A lot of families serve hybrid American and Colombian foods for the holidays, but don't ask for stuffing or mashed potatoes—only rice in most houses. Definitely expect: *arepas* (thick tortillas made with a corn flour called *masa*), *empanadas* (also made with *masa*), and *buenuelos* (fried cheese balls) with hot Colombian cocoa for breakfast. Yum!"

**WHO WILL YOU BE SITTING NEXT TO?:**

"You never know who will show up for dinner, but everyone is invited—friends, friends of friends, etc., and they all stop by to eat and drink. If you don't have a knack for remembering faces, just make a toast to everyone."

**A TRADITION PETA WOULD NOT APPROVE OF:**

"Some relatives might head up to a traditional Colombian ranch (*finca*) for Christmas. For dinner they roast a pig, but before the pig is cooked, they chase it around the party. Everyone then smears pig's blood on themselves. You can probably thank *aguardiente* (a strong, clear Colombian rum–like alcohol) for that lovely custom!"

**YOUR WINNING MOVE:**

"Don't be shy or on a diet. Be ready to eat, drink *aguardiente*, and dance the night away to traditional Colombian *cumbia* and *vallenato* music—you can't shake your ass to Bing Crosby."

**HOW TO BLOW IT FOREVER:**

"Jokingly ask if someone in his family is involved in a Colombian drug cartel. You will never be invited over again. Seriously."

**Italian In-Laws . . . *according to Stephanie, Philadelphia***

**TRUTHS:**

"Come hungry and be prepared to take leftovers, some basil, and a jar of peppers with you when you leave. And until you make tomato sauce that tastes just like theirs, you will never be fully accepted."

**BEHAVIORS FROM THE OLD COUNTRY:**

"When you leave, his grandma will give you some cash—which she removes from inside a hankie pinned to her bra."

**THE CRAZY RELATIVE AT THE TABLE WILL BE:**

"The unmarried virgin cousin who baked dozens of inedible *unbreakable* cookies for Christmas that you will be forced to eat—with a smile—for weeks."

**THINGS PECULIAR TO HIS FAMILY, BUT MAY NOT BE CULTURAL:**

"There are women in his family you may never see dressed in anything other than a housecoat and apron. This includes at your wedding."

**HOW TO BLOW IT FOREVER:**

"Ask for salt and pepper, which is the equivalent of tap dancing on the table while singing 'This food tastes like sh*t!'—in short, an outrage!"

**YOUR WINNING MOVE:**

"Come armed with cannoli or a nice ricotta cheesecake."

Still feeling culturally clumsy? Worried that your one verse of "Frere Jacques" won't cut it in your French-only in-law household? Here is a chart of useful words and phrases in a dozen languages. Translation: "Hey, we've so got your back, sista."

## Useful Phrases When In-Laws Don't Speak English

| Language | "Good morning" | "Thank you" | "Bimbo" | Phrases you don't want to hear |
|---|---|---|---|---|
| Spanish | Buenos días | Gracias | mujer joven | *Espero que no sea en serio.*<br>I hope that they're not serious. |
| Hindi | Su prabhat | Dhanyawaad | rundi | *Mein use kabhi muaf nahii karuungaa!*<br>I will never forgive him! |
| Mandarin | Zǎo | Xìe xie | Sān bā | *Nǐ xīn tài hēi le*<br>Your heart is black! |
| Yiddish | Ah gut morgen | A dank aych | tsatskele | *A klog is mir.*<br>Woe is me. |
| Arabic | Sabaah al-khayr | Shukran | shlicke | *Tdh-fa el fuse ma fish Kahraba.*<br>The fuse went out and there is no electricity. |
| Italian | Buon giorno | Grazie | donnaccia | *Non somiglia niente a Isabella Rossellini!*<br>She looks nothing like Isabella Rossellini! |
| Portuguese | Bom dia | Obrigado | pessoa | *Burro que nem uma porta.*<br>Stupid as a door. |
| French | Bonjour | Merci beaucoup | pute | *J'ai invité son ancienne copine, Annie, pour le dessert.*<br>I invited Annie, his old girlfriend, for dessert. |

| Language | "Good morning" | "Thank you" | "Bimbo" | Phrases you don't want to hear |
|---|---|---|---|---|
| Russian | Dobroye utro | Spasiba | pustushka | *Doctor mne skazal shto ya uzhe ne zarazna.* The doctor told me it is no longer contagious. |
| Greek | Kalimera | Efharisto | hazie | *Miyazee Turkala.* She looks like a Turk! |
| Irish | Maidin mhaith | Go raibh maith agat | striapach | *Go lagaí galar tógálach do chroí.* May an infectious disease weaken your heart. |
| German | Guten Morgen | Danke schön | Häschen | *Wer hat gefurzt?* Who farted? |

## The 365 Days of Holidays

If Hallmark has a card to commemorate an occasion, your in-laws want to celebrate it with you. They may not tell you this, but they're thinking it. Why? Because all holidays, big or small, are ultimately about family. Expect pressure in some form on:

**Arbor Day:** Not just for trees anymore, your sister-in-law has a gallery opening . . . in Des Moines.

**Martin Luther King Jr. Day:** Your in-laws say: "Why not come down to Florida and bring the grandkids? It's only twelve hours round-trip and you get a whole day in Boca."

**4th of July:** Your in-laws are going to Atlantic City and you're invited to watch Uncle Larry do body shots off the waitress! Or off of you!

The list goes on and on. In short, it doesn't matter if you strap reindeer antlers to you head, hang lanterns for Chinese New Year, or blow out birthday candles, holidays are about spending time with family. Just not with your own.

## My **Bleeping** In-Law!

Just when you thought you couldn't handle anything else during the holidays, below is your own personal "release valve." Now, you can pop your cork safely. No one will lose an eye. There will be no hard feelings. In the spirit of holiday sharing and venting, find the perfect words and fill in the blanks:

For Thanksgiving, my ________ *(adjective)* mother-in-law is such a ________ *(noun that rhymes with "itch")* when it comes to ____ *(verb)* ing and ____ *(verb)* ing. I should tell her to "________________ *(something you do with your lover)*" when she asks me to ____ *(verb)*. Someday when she is old and ________ *(adjective)*, I will ________________ *(professional wrestling move)* her wheelchair off a ____ *(noun)* and reclaim my inner peace.

My ________ *(adjective)* sister-in-law's holiday cooking is ________ *(adjective)*. Unfortunately, I'm lactose-intolerant. Her smoked turkey, shrimp bisque, and ____ *(nouns)* are soaked in butter, ____ *(noun)*, and cheese. If I refuse, she becomes a ____ *(noun)*, pouting and ____ *(verb)* ing. To make peace, I volunteer to ____ *(verb)* the dirty dishes. Only a few more days, and I'll be back in my ____ *(noun)*. Must stay calm!

This year, in an effort to be evenhanded, my ________________ *(nickname for your sweetie)* and I celebrated Mother's Day with both mothers. We bought them matching ________ (item from SkyMall). Unfortunately, my mother-in-law, Mrs. ________ (schoolyard taunt), opened her gift, and it had ________ (past-tense verb) during shipping. Of course, my ______ (adjective)-acious mother-in-law made a ______ (adjective) face and yelled: "________ (Expression)! You *paid* for this?" She wouldn't let us live it down. I wish we had given her a pile of ______ (bodily fluid) instead.

For Valentine's Day, ____________ (nickname for your partner) supposedly planned to ________ (romantic activity) on St. Lucia with me. Instead, we're eating ______ (breakfast cereal) for dinner in ________ (depressing U.S. city) with his recently dumped sister. She's spent all morning ___ (verb)ing and talking about her ________ (barnyard animal) of a(n) ______ (adjective) husband. My ____________ (less flattering nickname for partner) can't say no to his family in their times of need. Hey girl? ________ (hazardous street sign)!

This year, we hosted July 4th at our place. Unfortunately, my brother-in-law felt our home was lacking—even though we had homemade ______ (plural noun) and frosty ______ (beverage) for everyone. Only if our walls were blanketed with giant photos of ______ (plural nouns) and ______ (plural noun), would he think it's festive enough. Apparently, doing ______ (dance move) near the grill, painting your ______ (body part) red, white, and blue, and singing ____________ (John Cougar Mellencamp song) is a July 4th requirement.

6

# bon voyage!

## Sunblock, secretive sex, and the art of vacationing with in-laws

EXCERPT FROM THE AUTHOR'S DIARY:

*I'm in the bathroom. This is my first moment alone in 36 hours, because I'm on a ski vacation with my in-laws. At 6:45 this morning, my father-in-law kicked down the bedroom door and practically shook me awake because "it was going to be a great powder day." I know what today will bring: Uncle Marty will tell another story about his colon surgery with his mouth full of corn muffin. My mother-in-law will take another photograph of me in the lodge with my hair frozen in a side ponytail. Right now, my in-laws are in the garage loudly making sense of why-god-why I'm not out on the ski mountain: "Was it the eggs? Does she need Imodium AD?" Leave me! Go on without me! Why can't the herd leave one sheep behind?*

## Sit Back, Relax

In preparation for your trip, you get your bangs cut, do the laundry, and find a dog sitter. Now, it's midnight and you're lying in bed with racing thoughts: Is one bathing suit enough? Is the iPod charged? Will you need nasal jelly? Why Disney World, *why*?

You fall asleep. You wake up. You drink a glass of water, worrying that tomorrow will begin *Weekend at Bernie's* redux. Where you play the part of Bernie, a corpse rigged with pulleys and wires controlled by your in-law family.

Remember, these are the same people who on a trip to Mexico said, "Oh my, just look at all the poverty! Here, Hank, take a picture of me with the poverty." The same people who leave cameras in restaurants and kids in stores. But you are neither a camera nor a child. You'll be fine.

After all, you're going on a vacation! Relish that you don't have to go to the emergency branding meeting on Monday. You don't have to clean your apartment. And, you don't have to cook dinner for a few nights. Bon voyage!

## Ghosts of Vacations Past

Your in-laws have been vacationing for decades. Some trips were fabulous, some were not so fabulous. You've already heard some of your significant other's previous vacation horror stories:

- The 1987 Colonial Williamsburg debacle when your partner got his arms stuck in the pillory for three hours
- The Sugarbush, Vermont, condo rental fire that left your in-laws in a Denny's wearing their Michigan Business School pajamas at 2 AM

"I went to Italy with my in-laws, including my grandmother-in-law. She complained the whole time, felt miserable that her various siblings alive and dead couldn't be there, too, and claimed that one glass of wine made her sick for a week. Then when we returned home she never stopped talking about how wonderful it had all been."

DREA, TRENTON

"My brother-in-law gave his credit cards to the government official in the security line at the Havana, Cuba, airport, because the official said he needed to write down all of the numbers."

SHEILA, SAVANNAH

"My in-laws and fiancé were rendezvousing in the Caribbean for five days. All of us were flying from different cities. Well, I arrived fine. They did not. Snowstorms closed their airports. The resort staff wouldn't let me check in because I have a different last name from my in-laws!"

LILY, PARK CITY

"I accidentally swore in front of my four-year-old nephew. Of course, he dropped the F-bomb the entire vacation. It was awkward, because where did he learn it? Hmm?"

NIKKI, TOPEKA

"My uncle-in-law asked me to play copilot on his seaplane. Of course, I jumped at the chance! What I didn't expect is that he buzzed the beach as low as 70 ft. I should have seen it coming. He was a pilot for the Blue Angels."

MARISSA, TAMPA

- The Club Med trip to Nevis Island where the staff rioted, the pool was bright green, and a cow wandered into your in-laws' ground-floor bedroom

Regardless of what surprises are in store for you, one thing is certain: your in-laws will try to pump you for information about you, your partner, and your future together. They will attempt to accomplish this by peeling you away from the pack using a technique called "divide and conquer." Mongol generals implemented it, and your in-laws have perfected it.

- *At Gate 16, Chicago O'Hare Airport:* Your mother-in-law can't find her reading glasses. She asks you to hang back and help her look. While you pat down the chairs and dirty carpets, she asks you how you and her son met. You realize then that he neglected to tell her you met during a beer-pong tournament (which you won).
- *At the Golden Sands Hotel in Miami:* Your in-law wants to show you the gorgeous sunset from the end of the pier—alone.
- *In El Yunque rain forest, Puerto Rico:* You're on a gorgeous misty hike in paradise, and your in-law stumbles on a loose rock. You stop to offer a helping hand and get hit with "Curtis. Is that a Jewish name?"

Whatever the question, you, like a baby seal about to be clubbed, stare ahead in silence. What you really need is a go-to conversation hijacker to lead your in-laws in another direction. After a leg-cramping drive or hours spent inhaling that strange odor in the recycled airplane air, you're off your game. You're vulnerable. So, when your in-laws start to really probe, you whip out:

- An *US Weekly*—who doesn't love a bad photo of Julia Roberts grocery shopping? Or *USA Today*'s colored weather map of an advancing cold front. They'll be busy for hours.
- A travel backgammon set, a deck of cards, or Uno. They won't have time to contemplate your uterus as they frantically try to combat your double-reverse wild card strategy. "Uno!" Motherf***ers!
- Sudoku. Go ahead. Hand candy to a baby. Hours later, your in-law will be dazed and drooling from a Sudoku-induced high.

No matter the mode of transport, they will make it appear as if circumstance separated you and yours. It wasn't a freak accident that everyone suddenly developed night blindness, forcing one of you to helm each car. Don't fall for the fake pumps, be blindsided by the pick and rolls, or shocked by the power plays. Transportation is a crucial zone of vulnerability; stay on offense. Enjoy a competitive advantage with this sneak peek at your in-law family's "playbook."

The in-law family vacation is a rite of passage. It's the wisdom-tooth surgery of dating. Some people recover quickly; others suffer in agony for weeks.

You must know the game plan before you step foot on the field. Are you a first-string player in the in-law family or just a benchwarmer? Not all guests are created equal: girlfriends aren't asked to do the group laundry; fiancées don't have to babysit; but wives are expected to give up their seat on the boat in Venice because they're already "family" and thus can be trampled on accordingly.

## The In-Law Vacation Playbook

| The Play | How Your In-Laws Implement It | The Defense |
|---|---|---|
| The Minnesota Spread | Your brother-in-law relinquishes his exit row seat to your 6'4" sweetie.<br>The pilot announces a delay. Your brother-in-law, now seated beside you, confesses that he's bisexual and no one else knows. | Dramamine.<br>Dramamine.<br>Dramamine.<br>In-flight movie.<br>Dramamine. |
| The Tallahassee Twister | In all the mayhem of crying kids, lost maps, stolen baggage, and missing insulin, you ended up in the other car alone with his dad.<br>This could be the longest two hours of your life. | Chug a big gulp. Inhale a Cheetos bag. Pop prunes.<br>Scream for a bathroom break. Then, rearrange. |
| Warner's Skirt Split | Your father-in-law insists the "men" load the car onto the ferry, while the "ladies" enjoy the sun deck. | Remind him that he's spent too many years parking the car.<br>It's time for him to enjoy the glory of the sea. |
| The Quarterback Sneak | You sister-in-law selects a 4 PM train. Your husband often works late.<br>He misses it. It's just you and your in-law. | Sit in the "quiet car." |

**The Key:**

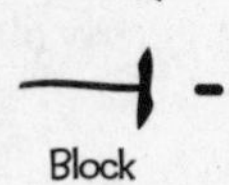

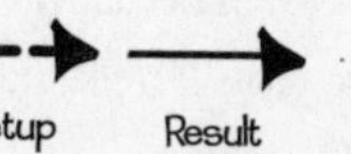

With great respect comes greater responsibility. Look at the chart below to foresee your player ranking.

**Not All Guests Are Created Equal**

| Trip | Girlfriend | Fiancée | Wife |
|---|---|---|---|
| 1 week at Canyon Ranch, Tucson | You weren't invited. No ring, no all-inclusive resort. | You feel guilty about having a resort spa treatment even though your in-laws offered. | You have a massage and a pedi, and put them both on the family credit card. |
| 4-day group tour of New York City | You sleep in a room with Grandma-in-law and her pet schnauzer, Bob. | You sleep in a room with sister-in-law. | You sleep in the same room with your man. |
| Weekend at the Russian River, Calif., house | After dinner, your plate is cleared. They're trying to impress you. | After dinner, you clear the plates. You're trying to impress them. | You cook dinner. Nobody's impressed. |
| Sun Valley, ski condo 6 days/5 nights | You rent skis. | You borrow skis. | Your in-laws gave you skis as a wedding gift. |
| 1 week in the London "apartment swap" | In the morning, you ask if there's coffee. | You're offered coffee in the morning. | You buy the coffee. For everyone. And scones. |

## In-Law Vacation Study Guide

Here are five typical in-law vacation itineraries to study and strategize from. It's one thing to keep your head above water for a plane flight; it's another to survive a weeklong in-law trip to the smallest house ever built on the isle of Nantucket. So hunker down beneath that germy airplane blanket. Catch some shut-eye. You'll need it.

### The Family Lake House

**Location:** Bass Lake, California
**Duration:** 5 days, 4 nights
**Who's going?**

Father-in-law (57)—runner; semiretired stockbroker; *West Wing* fanatic

Mother-in-law (56)—runner; amateur chef who packs her own spices

Brother-in-law (26)—runner; plumber; grows pot in his garden

Brother-in-law's girlfriend (25)—runner; pretty; obviously anorexic though claims to have "wheat allergies"

**Highlights:**

- ♥ The seven-mile daily "family fun run" that's not fun
- ♥ Your brother-in-law purchasing a hemp poncho at the crafts fair
- ♥ Your brother-in-law's girlfriend asking, "What's a 'blue state'?"
- ♥ Your brother-in-law trying to save you money by fixing the transmission in your 1994 Jeep Wagoneer, which instead leads to spending three hours and $175 at Pep Boys

**Sleeping arrangements:**

You and your brother-in-law's girlfriend share a room; however, she spends most nights in a tent in the driveway with brother-in-law.

**Where you have sex:**

In the Jeep Wagoneer—especially now that you can't drive it until Pep Boys gets that pinion crush sleeve in.

**What you're doing at midnight before you leave for vacation:**

Searching the Internet for photos of poison ivy, wolf spiders, and coyotes.

Welcome to the family house at Bass Lake! Smell that crisp air. Admire the yellow butterflies fluttering. Before unloading your luggage, prepare yourself for the following truths about the lake house:

**Truths About Your In-Laws' Lake House**

1. "Soft" mattress is a nice way of saying "lumpy" mattress.
2. Clothes dried on the "rustic" clotheslines are sticky with sap, and *What is that? Bird poop?*
3. No matter how many sweatshirts you wear, you're freezing.
4. You will find your partner's baby teeth in the nightstand drawer.
5. Colossal, prehistoric moths live in your lampshade.

## Ah, the Lake Life

You awaken to find your mother- and father-in-law breast-stroking away in the lake. Your brother-in-law, his girlfriend, and your fiancé dive like dolphins. This is your first introduction to clannish behavior. They're too afraid to admit the lake is painfully frigid.

From the porch you wave. Wearing your sweater and trying to eat cereal with gloves on, you pretend you don't hear: "Get your bathing suit! C'mon in! It's so refreshing!"

An hour later, you're toeing the water. From the surface, it's pristine, but the slimy lake bottom is another story. You rid your mind of the lake eel, the water snake, and the snapping turtle. You've also chosen to ignore the dead fish floating beneath the dock—the ones your father- and brother-in-law didn't properly de-hook last night, and now they're belly up. Nice.

### The Rope Swing of Death

There she is. She's gorgeous with her rotting rope, five wooden steps nailed to a tree trunk, and elevated platform (about 10 to 15 feet high) begging you to "please, fracture your arm."

It doesn't matter that rope swings are for bored ninth graders who can't drive to the movies. For the moment, you're not a global brand manager at Chanel. You're a sissy-pants who won't dive off the rope swing. With 6,000 cannonballs of training under their belts, your in-laws have perfected the art of the rope swing and might share their secrets. To avoid rope burn, stay on their good side.

### Big Boy Lake Toys

In the name of exploration, you and your partner join his brother and girlfriend for a leisurely canoe ride out to the small rock island. You're the first to step out and discover it's coated in a thick layer of goose poop. So much for that picnic.

From the dock, your mother-in-law lounges in the paddleboat; it looks fun and relaxing. When you try it, you find yourself stranded in the middle of the lake with a back spasm. After you nearly get run over by the neighbors on their Jet Skis, you realize that paddling is for chumps.

So the next day, you and yours rent Jet Skis and encounter the scary lakeside neighbors again—who steer straight for you, fling beer cans into the lake, and call you an S.O.B for getting in their way yesterday.

Finally, you return to the rope swing. And to simpler times.

### Kelly's Pancake Buffet

For twelve years, your in-laws have made the pilgrimage to a breakfast mecca. You've heard about "all you can eat" with

> **Mr. and Mrs. Clean**
>
> If your in-laws' vacation home is "dust free" and everything is at 90-degree angles, you're in the presence of neat freaks. How do you vacation with such in-laws?
>
> - Know that on the last morning of the trip you will wake up to the vacuum cleaner banging against your bedroom door. Your mother-in-law will be yelling about the trash. And your father-in-law will be outside shaking seat cushions. All before 7 AM.
> - Even if a cleaning service is part of the rental house agreement, your in-laws will clean. Confused, you ask: "Why are you cleaning if there's a hired maid service?" Your in-laws will respond: "Well, we don't want them to think we're slobs, now do we?"

"bacon miles high" and "the most delicious waffles in the world." You expect to see Food Network critics falling on the floor in buttery ecstasy, twitching in sugar comas. For "the best breakfast, like, ever," it's really nothing to write home about.

This is a ritual. Identify it. Accept it. Don your anthropological hat and observe their tribal tradition. There are certain things that societies have done for centuries. Cave drawings. Basket weaving. All-you-can-eat buffet breakfasts. Timeless.

> "My in-laws insist on washing the dishes after every meal. Apparently, I take too long to wash the dishes. I don't know if it's a conservation thing or what, but

they don't actually clean the plates. There's always food stuck to them. Don't get me started on the backs of the plates—they're gross."

BENITA, KANSAS CITY

### Tales from the Trash Can

Billy Joe, your in-laws' parrot, flies unencumbered around the house leaving "presents" in his wake. The penne noodle that fell off your plate five months ago is still on the dining-room floor. When you're the neat freak, how do you vacation with in-laws who are not?

- Gently offer to do the dishes, take out the trash, or try that vacuum cleaner that everyone thinks is broken. If your in-laws protest because "this is vacation and you shouldn't clean," do it when they're freezing their nuts off in the lake.
- Resist the urge to trail behind your brother-in-law with a bottle of Fantastik and a paper towel. It's painful to see him spill Welch's Grape Soda on the couch cushions and weakly mop it up with a shoe. Just look away and silently chant: "I am not sticky. I am not sticky."
- Neatly put away your valuable belongings. If the Nick Hornby book you're reading is important, don't leave it on the coffee table. Best-case scenario: it ends up as a coaster. Worst-case scenario: it ends up in the lake.

## THE ALL-INCLUSIVE BEACH RESORT

**Location:** Grand Wailea Resort Hotel, Maui, Hawaii
**Duration:** 6 days, 5 nights
**Who's going?**

Father-in-law (57)—recent divorcé; calls Viagra "vitamin V"; determined to make up for "lost time"

Father-in-law's new girlfriend (only 7 years older than you are)—dental hygienist; just upgraded from B to D cup; never misses her Tae Bo in the morning

**Highlights:**

- Your in-law sticking his hand in the back pocket of his girlfriend's jeans
- Turning down the invitation from your in-law and his girlfriend to go to a nude beach
- Your in-law and his girlfriend French-kissing during the luau pig roast
- Constantly agreeing with your partner that his dad's girlfriend is too young
- His dad grabbing you for an overly long hug and saying please call him "Dr. Lei"

**Sleeping arrangements:**

You share a room, which is great, except your in-law and his ladyfriend are right next door, constantly going for "the nookie." Even earplugs and the roar of the Pacific can't drown it out. Somehow your young love gets a lot older, watching *Law & Order* on high volume in bed.

**What you're doing at midnight before you leave:**

Reintroducing fruits for your second stage of the South Beach Diet.

**What you pack:**

Tankinis, condoms.

**What you should have packed:**

*The Father/Son Dynamic* by Dr. Leffer.

Aloha! The airport taxi pulls up to a gorgeous hotel—a place that *Travel & Leisure* tagged as "the dreamer's paradise." You tie up your hair and expose your neck and shoulders for the hibiscus lei. *Ahh, the island breeze.* Mahalo!

You're impressed that your in-law is taking life by the horns. Some people deal with divorce by gaining twenty pounds and reading Proust; others deal with it by dating dental hygienists and going to Hawaii. Now, you've got front-row seats on the Mid-Life Crisis Express.

Going away with your partner is a wonderful opportunity for everyone to bond and for your father-in-law to make up for cheating on your sweetie's mom. Unfortunately, in his new-found zest for life, he views this trip less like a vacation with his child and more like an extended double date. When Dr. Lei bangs on your door for "a spare jimmy," there's going to be trouble.

### Day One: The Hobie Cat as Metaphor

You wake up and admire the sunlight glinting off the surf from the lanai. Over a delicious group breakfast, your in-law spots a pink and yellow sail gliding across the turquoise water. Moments later, you're squeezed into an orange life vest and clutching a Hobie Cat for dear life. Your in-law's recent divorce has not only made him adventurous with ladies, but with life and the lives of others.

The world is your water park. A few high G-force turns take your breath away—the speedometer reads 35 mph. You point out dolphins and sea turtles. This is glorious!

Exactly ten minutes later, a "rogue wave," "unforeseen reefs," or "pilot error" capsize you. And whether you know it or not, your whole vacation has turned upside down, too. Years of childhood rage in your partner surface. He screams, "Dad, you're such an a-hole!" Yelling escalates, while you bob up and down on the waves. You hope sharks prefer silicone to you.

Tension thickens as you towel off in the rescue boat. What started off as a sun-dappled day of adventure has ended up sodden and sulking. There is trouble in paradise.

### Days Two, Three, and Four: The Family Pickle

You think the fight will blow over. So you hole up in the hotel room with your beloved waiting for an apology from your father-in-law. But there's only so long you can entertain yourself. Somewhere between resetting the room safe and taking artsy photos of trees from the lanai, you're secretly grateful that Housekeeping has tossed you out.

Unfortunately, the only thing your sweetie wants to do is hit the indoor gym—for hours. He needs space. And endorphins. That's okay; you need sun.

You figure you're strong enough to go it alone. What better way to get to know Dad and What's-Her-Name than to play third wheel for a while? You survived the lecture on the importance of flossing, and were supportive when Dr. Lei got his ear pierced, but hanging out while they make out is not an option. Nor is joining your honey's one-man iron-pumping pity party. So you're left with choice number three.

**How to Excuse Yourself from Awkward Situations**

1. Feign food poisoning. Tell them that the fish taco wasn't a good idea.
2. Yawn excessively and declare jet lag is sending you to bed.
3. Ask a waiter to whisper in your ear, and then politely say: "Please, excuse me. They need me."

4. Pretend you recognize your Finnish pen pal, Ritva, and chase after her.
5. Blink wildly. Drop to your hands and knees and look for a "lost contact" (you don't wear contacts).

Welcome to singles life at the resort! You sign up for windsurfing lessons. Afterward, you learn your sweetie ordered the entire *Lord of the Rings* trilogy On Demand. You opt for a group snorkel outing, read beneath the banyan tree, and join hatha yoga in the beachside pavilion. It's only after the sunset horseback-riding trip, the one where the group nicknames you "Poopy" because your horse does his business the whole time, that you hit your limit. You're lonely. Isolated. Hours away from making friends with a volleyball and naming it Wilson.

## Day Five: Taking Matters into Your Own Hands

Hell, you didn't fly six hours and go on a diet to waste away in the lap of luxury tangled in a family tug-of-war. If they want to argue and hate each other and bring up years of resentment and disappointment, they can do it like a normal family—at Christmas, for chrissakes. Not in Hawaii! Here are a few tips to diffuse the tension and discord when your sweetie and your in-law are fighting:

1. **The Meddling Dr. Phil:** Set a trap. Meet them at Pu'u Keka'a, the famed black rock, and declare that they're not getting off that damn mountain until they resolve this fight. Launch into a monologue about how life is short. People get hit by Hobie Cats! Sometimes there isn't time to say good-bye!

2. **The Direct Dr. Phil:** Stage a family intervention. Sign the boys up for the Halekula doubles tennis tournament and let their joint competitive spirit heal them. Your sweetie can take his aggression out on the court and set up easy shots for Bob and Marge from Pasadena to peg his dad at the net.
3. **The Erratic Dr. Phil:** Take one for the team. Contradict everything anyone says. Whine. Demand to go to an authentic Hawaiian restaurant and then bitch and moan that there's pineapples on everything. Wear your "I Hate Poi" T-shirt. Draw all their hate and irritation toward yourself. Eventually your sweetie will forgive, but with any luck your in-law will think you're such a pain in the ass that he'll never invite you on vacation ever again.
4. **The Angry "Tiki God" Dr. Phil:** Violate a local deity, thereby causing an earthquake or tidal wave of angry retribution. Evacuation of the entire island is inevitable, thus cutting this vacation short.

None of these interventions is likely to heal all wounds. But short of dropping the L-bomb, the four of you will put the Hobie Cat behind you on the Wampanoag State Park hike. The last 30 hours of the Hawaiian trip are more like your travel agent promised. You and yours nap in a cabana, clink Amaretto fizz drinks, and make your own hotel room noise. If only you could remain on island time.

## The Rented Beach House

**Location:** Edgartown, Martha's Vineyard, Massachusetts
**Duration:** 4 days, 3 nights

**Who's going?**

Mother-in-law (52)—loves her boys, but from a safe distance; can't tolerate "spicy" foods

Father-in-law (54)—Partner in old-line Boston law firm; bird-watcher; yachtsman

Dog-in-law (???)—very old; on death's door; named Chester Chesterfield III

**Highlights:**

- Drinking Earl Grey tea with lemon until 4 PM and then switching to gin
- Throwing a ball at Chester and afterward learning he's blind
- The lack of concern for a Category 5 hurricane, Amelia, brewing offshore; "My great-granddaddy built this place and it won't blow away now."
- Your mother-in-law calling everyone and everything she doesn't like "nouveau riche"
- Regretting telling your in-laws: a) about the time as a child you did "number two" in the ocean and it washed up on shore; and b) that your parents' first language was not English

**Sleeping arrangements:**

Happily, you two have your own room; however, the walls are decorated with creepy portraits of family members from generations of yore.

**Where you have sex:**

Anywhere but this room because a hundred eyes staring at your naked butt is a total buzz kill.

**What you're doing at midnight before you leave:**

Nair-ing

**What you packed:**

*Star Magazine*

**What you should have packed:**

*Town & Country*

You're admiring the brass mallard duck knocker when the front door swings open. Your well-manicured, white-haired mother-in-law eyes you up and down. You lean in for a warm hug. She recoils from your affectionate touch. Then your partner's dad strolls around the side of the house holding a scotch tumbler. He's six feet tall and a soft talker. Actually, all of them are. Is someone sleeping? Why are they whispering?

The house is decorated with crisscrossed boat paddles, nautical ropes, and gingham pillows. Not your taste, but that's fine! You catch yourself in a seashell-crusted mirror and realize your flip-flops, Parrot Bay Rum tank top, and cornrows don't match the decor. You start to feel like a big piece of "beach trash" that blew into their house.

Tentatively, you hand them your housewarming present, a trout-shaped stapler and frog tape dispenser. Who wouldn't want fun desktop companions? Answer: your in-laws. They have no place for such warm gifts in their ice castle by the sea.

Finally, someone mentions supper. You love barbecue! They pause. They don't have a BBQ; they have a grill. And since today is Friday, they'll be eating fish.

Finally, over dinner, with the help of Mr. Johnny Walker and Mr. Tom Collins, your in-laws thaw. You tell yourself: the glass is half full! Your in-laws aren't housebound WASP-bots. She gardens compulsively. He plays squash. The next morning at the breakfast table, as you spread $10.95 fig and almond jam on your corn muffin, you endure more conversations about:

a) Your partner's lacrosse, rugby, and crew days
b) The country club and the "controversial" new lax membership requirements
c) British royalty; Nat King Cole; Druidic lore; Freud; Chaucer; garden arrangements; what is gauche; Boston's Beacon Hill; alumni activities at Wellesley and the upcoming lecture at "the other little Ivy, Amherst"

You've seen *Survivor.* Remember, someone gets voted off after a silly test of will. You'll be damned if they'll intimidate you. Make you feel like you're less well read, worldly, and abreast of polo rules, even if it's true! You're not leaving, so they can find a "nice" girl for their son and by "nice," they mean "a girl with Anglo-Saxon features whose dad has influence in the Senate."

### The A/C Divide

Clearly, your in-laws don't sweat; it's because they're frigid people. But their refusal to use A/C feels decidedly hostile. After positioning three fans in your bedroom, the backs of your knees

**How do you deal if your in-laws refuse to use air-conditioning?**

- Go to the mall or any air-conditioned store, movie theater, or supermarket. No, you don't have to buy anything. Just stare longingly at the Stouffer's frozen pizzas. You could be one of them some day.
- Invest in Nike, Adidas, or Reebok sweat-wicking tank tops and shorts.
- Take cold showers. Go into the ocean. It's like mile 15 of the marathon. It's perfectly acceptable to dump a glass of water over your head in the living room.

**How do you deal if your in-laws blast the air-conditioning?**

Like many menopausal women and those living with menopausal women, your in-laws live like Eskimos, keeping the thermostat at 60 degrees. What can you do?

- Save room in your luggage for an extra sweatshirt that you can wear around the house. If the dress code is formal, make it cashmere. Better yet, if your in-laws own the vacation home, stash a sweater in a closet so it's there, welcoming you with its woolly embrace year in and year out.
- Hot cocoa is a girl's best friend. That, and tea, coffee, and especially "Irish coffee." If the ice from the ubiquitous G&Ts is making your teeth chatter, offer to mix your in-laws a hot toddy; hey, you're killing so many birds with one stone here.
- Heating pads are not just for menstrual cramps. You can surreptitiously plug in when you're alone in the den, turning the pages of *In Style* with one hand while the other one thaws under your butt.

are still sticky. Suffering is in their blood. Did I say suffering? Wait, that's for the oppressed people of the world. I mean "being tough" and "riding it out" and "working hard." These people descended from the pilgrims. A little heat? Nah, that's nothing.

## The Outdoor Shower

Your in-laws have crossed the line and just plain lied to you. They proclaim: "Oh, the outdoor shower! It's fantastic." Of course, you had to experience this for yourself.

You thought you were alone in the outdoor shower, yet

you feel watched. In fact, you are—by eight sets of eyes. Tall spiders. Short spiders. Brown spiders. Black spiders. You successfully negotiate with the one perched on the faucet and rinse the others down the drain. But one humongous hairy arachnid remains. He isn't fazed that you're two hundred times his size.

Note that your in-laws will never once use the outdoor shower themselves. There is a distinct smell of Pert Plus and Irish Spring emerging from the master bath at all times. No, fair daughter-in-law, the outdoor shower is for those guests who aren't a part of the biological bunch.

What should you do? Pack flip-flops or make your sweetie guard the door as you speed-clean in the Royal Bathroom. Then trap a spider and release it in their lair. Who's got arachnophobia now?

### Family Traditions

Your in-laws' favorite pastime appears to be: drinking and smoking cigars, followed by more drinking, and sometimes, driving. Scotch on the rocks. Gin and tonics. Whatever your poison, it's in the bar, and the bottles, unlike your in-laws, are neither old nor dusty.

Your father-in-law offers to pick you up after you see a movie. That seems thoughtful until his Saab swerves up to the theater. Your trip home involves a detour over a sand dune because he saw one of "those rabbits that are ruining the garden."

What can you do? Offer to show your father-in-law a shortcut home and slide into the driver's seat. Or take him out for more drinks and get him so sloshed that he's laughing as you strap him to the backseat. Either way, someone with a B.A.C. lower than 2.0 needs to get behind the wheel.

**I've Never Heard of**
***The Da Vinci Code***

Hey, cruise director? Sit down! Recommending novels, movies, or restaurants on in-law vacations can be a bust. Inevitably, your rental choice of *Seabiscuit* bores them to tears and the local fish restaurant you select (the one with the rave reviews) gives everyone the Norwalk virus. Sometimes, it's best to be bland, boring, and unopinionated—for once!

### If You Can't Beat Them, Join Them

This weekend wasn't exactly what you hoped for. And you know there are more weekends like this in your future. Here are some tricks to keeping your wits:

1. *Your partner, the spokesperson:* You and yours want to bow out of yachting. Let him drop the news. If you are constantly the bearer of bad news and broken plans, they'll assume it's always your idea. Have him do some of the dirty work.
2. *If you're feeling like a Philistine (a word you had to look up):* Be confident. So you're not "old money" or even part of the larger category of "the Establishment." Who cares! You've got "a lot of personality" and must come from a "colorful family"—*whatever* that means.
3. *Reality check:* When the house is too much to handle, there's always coastline to stroll. Shells to skip. Surf shops and whaling exhibits to explore. You'll have to endure haughtiness within the confines of the beach house walls. Get used to it. Because like salmon returning to the same spawning site, your partner will return to the beach house

for the next fifty summers. Get on the bus, Gus. There's no way to fight it.

### The Italian Bus Tour

**Location:** Rome, Florence, and Tuscany
**Duration:** 7 days, 6 nights
**Who's going?**

Mother-in-law (55)—divorced; collector of decorative plates; always comments about "letting herself go" and how she used to fit into clothes your size

Sister-in-law (19)—wears Juicy Couture track suits; struggled with "the Freshman 15" this past year at Syracuse

Uncle-in-law (54)—owns successful construction company; constantly talks about the war on terror and why it's the right thing to do; he paid for the trip

Cousin-in-law (25)—hates her dad; wants only to read *Vogue* magazine and sulk

**Highlights:**

- Your uncle-in-law alerting airport security to a "suspicious-looking traveler"
- Constant comparisons of your food in Italy to the Olive Garden
- Your sister-in-law not knowing where the toilets are located in the Vatican and almost losing it in God's house
- Your uncle-in-law grabbing the microphone on the tour bus to tell a joke about the pope, a beaver, and a martini
- The British tour guide, Dexter, asking your uncle-in-law not to touch the microphone

**How you get there:**

You uncle-in-law books cheap flights to Florence, which is terrific, except for the layovers in New York, Hong Kong, and Berlin.

**Sleeping arrangements:**

You share a room with all the ladies

**Where you have sex:**

In the Uffizi

**What you're doing at midnight before you leave:**

Practicing your Italian, which is 90 percent hand gesturing and 10 percent phrases

**What you pack:**

Sturdy walking shoes

**What you should have packed:**

A freezer-storage-size baggie of Valium

To travel on motor coach is to travel like a king. It's like being on tour with the opening band for The Pulps. Who? Exactly.

For weeks, you've been daydreaming about being whisked from artistic masterwork to architectural gem. You almost taste the Chianti. And to think this trip is your uncle-in-law's treat! *Prego!*

Maybe you should have realized that your Italian adventure would be less *Under the Tuscan Sun* and more *National Lampoon's European Vacation*. It's your in-laws. These are people who can't go to Dairy Queen without it turning into a major international incident.

## Your Uncle-in-Law: The Class Clown

Within the first hour on the bus, your uncle-in-law nudges you to pass along his open bag of chips to your neighbor. So begins "the buffeteria" experience of the tour—the rampant and decidedly unhygienic passing around of food. Thanks, in-law. The bus reeks of Cool Ranch Doritos, soda, and flatulence.

Ably demonstrating that we never leave our second-grade selves behind, your in-law cracks a corny joke, no matter what historical spot or gorgeous landscape the group has gone to see. And there's only so much grabbing the microphone, singing, telling jokes, and inept celebrity impersonation that Dexter the tour guide can take.

One morning, your in-law closes the bus doors and won't let you on, to prove the point that you can't be late and delay the bus for the third day in a row. Tempers flare because Dexter has asked your uncle repeatedly not to touch the bus doors. Voices rise. Your uncle-in-law screams: "You'll be hearing from my travel agent!" He claims he's "had enough of this abuse" and that he "will not step foot back on the bus, so help me God."

You want to plead that you're not one of them and continue with the tour to the Siena for the Palio Festival. Then you glimpse your partner and realize there's a reason they call the

**In-laws traveling in Italy are a handful. Here are five useful phrases:**

| | |
|---|---|
| I'm sorry | *Mi dispiace* |
| Don't worry; I'll leave you a big tip | *Non preoccupar; gli lascerà una punta grande* |
| We'll be out of here soon | *Saremo da qui presto* |
| Please don't call the police | *Non telefonare prego la polizia* |
| He's got Tourette's syndrome | *Ha la sindrome del Tourette* |

mafia a family. *La cosa nostra*—your family is your own. You don't squeal. You're in this for life. And no one gets out alive. Standing on the curb, you watch the bus pull away along with your "perfect" Italian vacation.

### The Shopping Houdini

Shopping, for your mother-in-law, is about the art of vanishing. No matter the village size or what your plans are for the day, she finds an open-air flea market and evaporates. Before you know it, the afternoon is gone. Museums close. Exhibits shut down. You tap the shoulder of a brown-haired woman dressed in a fanny pack and silk blouse, but it's not your in-law. Where'd she go?

Releasing her into a *mercato* is akin to releasing a bargain hunter into Wal-Mart on Black Friday. Nothing screams "authentic Italian" like hand-painted porcelain plates with jolly farmers, Michelangelo, and the Tower of Pisa. Even if they're made in Taiwan, at least they were bought in Italy!

What can you do if your in-law must buy gifts for everyone she ever met?

- Talk about the fantastic souvenirs in the museum gift shops. You get to see Botticelli's *Birth of Venus* while she buys T-shirts. Everyone is happy.
- Gently remind her that what is "uniquely" Italian in today's global economy can be bought online. She may appreciate your efforts to save her (and you!) from returning home toting untold pounds of bubble-wrapped pottery.
- Redirect her. Encourage her to purchase gifts in one fell swoop. Send all the friends and relatives espresso beans from one factory. This way, they can't compare gifts stateside and determine who is your mother-in-law's "favorite."

### Your Sister-in-Law: The Time Suck

Your sister-in-law's 5 AM blow-dry sessions keep you from your beauty rest. Her excessive luggage creates deathtraps in the middle of the night. Her lengthy shower routine leaves you just enough time for a spit bath. Clearly, she's over-indulged.

No one scolds her for losing her *biglietto cumulativo* for all the museums, even though it was supposed to save money. Your most salient memory of the day in San Gimignano is not the history or the architecture; it's the Saga of Her Three-Inch Platform Espadrilles and the Tragic Sprained Ankle, which consumed everyone's afternoon.

She treats you and everyone else like personal assistants. Suddenly, it's your job to explain to a waiter the concept of lactose intolerance by mooing and miming nausea. She barely looks up from her nails and says, "Actually, I want eggplant!" You have no idea how you're going to mime *that* one.

When in Rome, how do you withhold from drowning your in-laws in the Trevi Fountain? Or overlook that they aren't "rising above the language barrier," constantly yelling in English at top volume?

- Create and distribute a daily itinerary of what you and your sweetie are doing. That way, when your uncle-in-law disappears into a discotheque or your sister-in-law takes five hours to put on eyeliner, everyone knows that there's an itinerary they're violating. Feel free to stick to it. See you at dinner! Or not!
- Deal with your in-law family's shifting moods and fickle behaviors with these two words: *Italian wine*. Rome wasn't built in a day. Nor was it built sober.
- Separate from the pack and explore. It may seem selfish in the moment, but you're only in Italy for a few days. If

you're worried about how you're perceived, send your in-laws a postcard *from* Italy, thanking them for the wonderful time. It'll be a welcome sight amid the Verizon bills and Sears catalogues when they get home.

Remember, *bella:* ultimately you're not going to see everything or do everything you wanted to do in Italy—for that you should have come alone. You're there to spend time with his family. And a year from now, when you receive an invitation from Stan-from-New-Jersey, to meet at his house for the bus tour reunion, laugh and enjoy when your uncle-in-law hijacks the mic at dinner. *Ciao!*

## The Ski Vacation

**Location:** Vail, Colorado
**Duration:** 1 week
**Who's going?**

Father-in-law (57)—former tight-end for Notre Dame; outruns, outplays, and outjumps "the young bucks"

Mother-in-law (55)—skies at 2 mph; wears red lipstick at all times

Brother-in-law (27)—is "stoked" about his new Atomic "Big Daddy" skis; leaves porn sites open on communal computer; has a big-boy appetite

Uncle-in-law (52)—plump version of father-in-law; is "the smart one" in the family

Cousin-in-law (24)—he "can't catch a ball"; paints, but "isn't gay"

Grandfather-in-law (77)—tough as nails; has skied in same green sweater since 1971; remembers Vail "when it was just a hill"

**Highlights:**

- Your artsy-fartsy cousin-in-law tearing his ACL on the first run of the day
- Gripping the steering wheel, white-knuckled, across the snowy highway passes of I-70 to buy Advil gelcaps
- Enjoying the wide, easy "green" slope with the other five-year-olds in your ski lesson
- Learning your grandfather-in-law's philosophy of marriage: "You make one mistake once and have to live with it for the rest of your life."
- Your in-laws gesturing unsuccessfully at the bottom of the ski trail that a snowcat is behind you

**How you get there:**

You fly, clutching the headrest of the seat in front of you as the prop plane pitches and falls.

**Sleeping arrangements:**

You share a room with your sweetie, but only because no one wants to sleep with the Snorer.

**Where you have sex:**

In your room before applying tiger balm. Never, never after.

**What you're doing at midnight before you leave:**

Checking the snow report and praying for blue sky and sunshine.

**What you pack:**

Skinny jeans.

**What you should have packed:**

Thermal fleece two-inch-thick black pants.

Welcome to the snowcapped mountains of Vail! Clydesdale horses pull families along cobbled streets. Snowdrifts blanket the imported Swiss architecture. And beyond "the beautiful people" sporting the Stetson hats, diamonds, and fur-lined vests looms the giant ski mountain rising into the crisp blue sky. Chairlifts whiz up and down the slopes. Gondolas disappear into the clouds. This place is *huge.*

You're so excited to lunch leisurely at Two Elk Lodge after a morning of relaxed skiing. Ah, the freedom of being in nature. You relish the privacy of sharing such a romantic hideaway with the person you love.

Maybe next year. This trip has already been planned for you. What you didn't see coming is that there will be no single moment alone, no single moment unaccounted for, and no single activity that you do away from the group for *the entire week*. Kidnap is a strong word. Intense camaraderie is nicer. Hoodwinked maybe.

### The Camp Director

Yes, you scanned the trip itinerary your mother-in-law sent you before you left. But you thought some things were optional. Sure enough, on the very first morning you awaken in alpine paradise, the itinerary blows its bugle.

*7:00 AM* Reveille

Your in-laws race up and down staircases. Full-blown panic sets in while looking for mittens, ski socks, lift tickets, and sunscreen. Is there a deadline? Why the rush?

You want to shout at your mother-in-law: "Ma'am, put down the pen, the glasses, and the wristwatch. Step away from the itinerary. Hands in the air!"

You're told it's a good idea to wear brightly colored ski clothing because weather changes quickly, so if caught in a blizzard, you'll be more visible. Your in-laws convince you to trade your stylish ski threads for a neon yellow 1984 Van-Halenesque ski suit they had lying around the house. Yes, it will be warm, but now you feel less like a snow bunny and more like a snow piñata. Somehow your hair already feathered itself and you're ready to *"Jump! Might as well jump!"*

All of this attention would be great if you knew how to ski. You fudged a little when you claimed you were an intermediate skier. Basically, you're better than a blind one-legged dog heading backward down the mountain.

| | |
|---|---|
| *7:30* AM | Discussion of which trails to ski together. You ask what time the hot chocolate break is. This is met with silence and awkward stares. |
| *8:00* AM | Your brother-in-law tells you that he's sleeping with three different women. |
| *8:30* AM | You throw your back out trying to get your ski boots on. |
| *9:00* AM | You and your partner are separated in the chairlift line. Your mother-in-law joins your chair. |
| *9:15* AM | At 70 feet in the air, your mother-in-law asks what your ten-year plan is. |

You stare off into space, admiring the treetops.

| | |
|---|---|
| *9:17* AM | She tells you being pregnant was the greatest joy in her life. |
| *9:18* AM | That she breast-fed your sweetie until he was two. |
| *9:19* AM | *When do you think you'll have kids?* |
| *9:20* AM | She didn't wait long after getting married. |
| *9:35* AM | You order a beer at the ski hut alone. |

Now you're sitting in the lodge adjusting to both the altitude and the attitude of your in-laws. Before you tear into your man about how misleading he was about this trip and its "relaxing vibe," there are a few more things you should accept about the ski vacation.

1. It takes twice as long to use the bathroom in ski boots.
2. The ubiquitous pine-scented hand soaps, air fresheners, and pillows will make you smell like you had a fight with an Old Spice deodorant and lost.
3. Are those real antlers on the bedside lamp? They feel real.
4. Each morning the group argues about who wants an "easy" ski day, and by easy, they mean "slum it with you."
5. Skiing brings out the worst in *most* couples, so if you finish each day still on speaking terms, you're ahead of the curve.

Okay, you made it into your clothes, onto a chairlift, and up the slope. Not bad. But, what you should really do is *take a lesson.* An instructor will teach you far better than your wannabe Bode Miller father-in-law. Like most beginners, you don't appreciate the advice to "shred the bunny slope."

### Diamonds, Diamonds Everywhere, but Not the Kind You Like

You're supposed to meet the whole gang for lunch at the mid-Vail lodge in 20 minutes. Your brother-in-law tells you that this trail, aptly named "Grim Reaper," is the fastest way down. You point to the "green" groomed beginner trail ten feet away. He shrugs. It will take too long.

Children barrel past. They aren't afraid. Maybe you'll be okay. But children also eat everything with ketchup; you can't trust them.

Off you go with wind at your back. Skis, boots, bindings, and your body are supposed to work in synchronicity . . .

somehow you fly into a six-foot snowdrift. Your skis are twenty feet above you and your poles are still tumbling down the trail. This will take hours. Your brother-in-law skies ahead to tell the lunch crowd you'll be late.

How do you carry on conversations with people who care only about snow reports? It's not easy. But here are some tricks to enjoy the ski trip when you're a novice and you've inherited a hyperactive ski family:

- **Don't be bullied:** End the schoolyard games. You can't be forced to ski into danger, as long as you're not physically tied to another person. Tell that bully to pick on someone his own size! And you want your lunch back!
- **Don't rationalize:** It doesn't make sense. It never will. Strap on planks of wood and point straight down an icy hill? It's simply Nordic madness. But your partner adores it. So, with each new day on the mountain, try to build positive experiences.
- **Rise and shine, early bird:** If you must follow your in-law down a mogul field because there's a wild lynx chasing you, do it early in the day before your legs are tired. Nothing says "dangerous" like weak leg muscles in the middle of a difficult trail at 3 PM while a wild lynx is chasing you.

### "Oh, So Tired"

Your calves burn. Your quads ache. You smell like a Bengay-abusing ninety-year-old woman, and feel like one because you want a walker, a heating pad, and maybe some ice cream. Most of all, you want a break from skiing. When you feel pressure to participate, work the ski scene.

Volunteer to wait in the lodge, save a table, mind the après-ski boots. Now you get to hang with your kind—the sedentary nonskiers of the mountain! Or on a "powder day," offer to grocery shop. It'll be a ghost town in Stop & Shop; the only people in the store either work there or have knee immobilizers.

Let your partner know when your in-laws are more than you can handle. Tell him to stop his dad from yapping his head off on chairlifts and volunteering your "expertise" to people like Dan-from-New-Mexico, because you know stocks better than anybody and Dan could use the money. Ask your sweetie to talk to his brother: you're tired of him waking you up from naps every day to play drinking games, claiming, "You'll sleep when you're dead, man."

With all of this madness, appreciate your in-laws when they're kind. They did your dirty ski laundry, lovingly separating your whites from your colors. Sure, it was a little creepy when they folded your clothes, including the lacy panties. Oh well.

It doesn't matter if you're attending a family reunion in Akron, Ohio, forced to eat more farm-stand corn than your stomach can handle, or at your sister-in-law's wedding in Los Cabos and asked to drive a crying bridesmaid to a Mexican strip mall for pantyhose.

You're family. You're one of them now. However, until you say "I do," you're not legally linked to your in-laws.

# 7

# for better, for worse, and forever

**It's not really *your* big day.**

EXCERPT FROM THE AUTHOR'S DIARY:

> *T-minus 2 months before the big day, and my in-laws are turning my wedding into a national AARP meeting. Someone might slip and break their hip walking to our wedding reception—do I have a plan for that? Uncle Max has cataracts—must I have an evening reception? What about renting oxygen tanks? A first-aid tent? And, why again, do I want a live band? It's hard for people to talk over that kind of racket. I've never met these aged guests, but I want to kick out their canes, curse their low bone density, and smash their reading glasses. I'll try to smile when Nana Sally from Palm Beach says she can't read the "small print" in the program. Screw her—it's my day.*

## Weddings: Blinded by Love

Congratulations. You found a good melon. Together you and your melon are basking in engagement-ring glow. You think: A wedding is just an elegant one-hour ceremony followed by a four-hour party—what could puncture a high this sublime?

Clearly, you've ignored the billion-dollar wedding industry; that's cool—you've had your blinders on these many years. It's only a short time until your normally carefree self spends hours yelling into your cell phone because:

- Your shy mother-in-law, whom you lovingly pulled into the wedding planning, finally pipes up and has only "one special request"—not to marry her son.
- Your father-in-law asks nonstop about the meat-carving station.
- Your brother-in-law wants to perform a trumpet solo of "Tequila."

There will be fisticuffs. There will be disappointments. Dear reader, there is a monster lurking in the wedding sea so terrifying it would make Jacques Cousteau pee his wetsuit. It's your in-laws. Their tentacles are not as ferocious as those of the mighty Kraken; but your in-laws will join you for brunch, politely kiss your cheek, slide their guest list of 250 people across the table, and order an iced tea while your world crumbles.

Whatever happened to "*you* are the bride"? It's *your* party? *Nobody puts baby in the corner*? Your in-laws ignore your wishes, blow past your deadlines, and worse, don't seem to hear a word you say. You're already on the edge; your in-laws push you over it.

It's okay to wish that your sweetie was raised by wolves. It would make wedding planning a lot easier. You could tie his entire extended family to a bobsled, give them kibble and a chew toy, and they'd be in doggie heaven. Accept it; saying "I do" is an infinitesimally small part of throwing the party of a lifetime for your in-laws.

> "So many mothers-in-law try to re-create the wedding day they didn't have. I can't tell you the times I've heard the verbal slip of my wedding . . . no, I mean my son's wedding."
>
> VANESSA, WEDDING PLANNER FROM DALLAS

For mothers-of-the-groom, it's often a learned pattern of abuse. It's the cycle of life. When they were young, their mothers-in-law hijacked their weddings. Now it's their turn.

## "The 10-Step Program" for Brides with In-Laws Anonymous (BWI)

Life's a bitch, kid. That's why there's country music. That's also why there's Brides with In-Laws Anonymous (BWI), the Living Recovery Program:

1. I admit that my efforts to involve my in-laws in the wedding have backfired.
2. I must stop crying, obsessively reshaping that one errant eyebrow hair, and instead turn to fellow brides for help.
3. Fellow brides who struggle with:

    - German in-laws who want Bavarian oompah, lederhosen, and dirndls at the ceremony.
    - Practical in-laws who married in a courthouse and believe this wedding is the financial equivalent of dousing cash in kerosene and setting it ablaze.

- Clueless in-laws who swap wedding invitations among their friends like tickets to a Knicks game *must* be in my life.

4. I will smile and politely consider the ridiculous suggestions my in-laws make:

    - Relocating the porta-potty a half mile away so the outdoor ceremony doesn't smell "like a cow pasture."
    - Inviting my sister-in-law to read her poetry during the wedding because she's so talented and "needs a break."
    - Incorporating a recommitment ceremony for my in-laws because "wouldn't that be neat?"

5. I will ask my fellow BWIs for the strength to forgive my in-laws' surprise baby-picture slideshow set to John Mellencamp's "Jack and Diane" at the reception.
6. I am ready to accept the moral support that BWIs will give me, because without it I will grind my teeth into a fine white powder. And the rehearsal dinner steak is too expensive to gum.
7. I will make a list of the mean things I've done, said, or *thought about saying* to my in-laws during my engagement (this includes the time I mailed my mother-in-law an anonymous note asking her not to cry with her mouth full) and burn it.
8. I will continue to make such lists and revise them daily, hourly, and if need be, every few minutes.
9. I promise not to elope to Belize. *Sigh.*
10. I appreciate what my fellow brides have done for me (e.g., keeping me from punting small fluffy dogs into the air) and I promise to mentor future brides who come to me in the same way.

"What?" you say. "But my in-laws are fine! Everything is FINE." Right. Today, you screamed at your yoga instructor and wanted to wipe that "smug" smile off Buddha's face. You must come to peace with the sticky situations where in-laws tend to wreak their most destructive wedding havoc. Below is the unspoken advice on how to be a guest at your in-laws' wedding and still feel as if it's your own.

## The Wedding Fund

If your in-laws want more at the wedding, then they should pay more. A side job at Marshalls would do wonders for the floral budget. See if you father-in-law is interested in applying.

Your in-laws have so many "needs": top-shelf alcohol, a live Peter Gabriel cover band, authentic Scottish bagpipes, and a choral rendition of "Danny Boy." The list never ends. All of this adds up to one thing: the dirty green monster called money. Mr. Cha-*Ching*.

There are several different financial models for weddings. Each one has its perks. And its oh-my-god-just-shoot-me-nows.

### Scenario 1: You're Paying for the Wedding

There are three reasons why you're paying for the wedding:

1. You've got all the dough:

   You're rated one of Barron's top 50 young bankers.
   Your grandfather invented Campbell's Soup.
   You matched 12-36-8-11-20 and won Powerball—payday!

2. City Hall = 100 bucks. No one is going to tell you what to do.
3. You're a finalist on *The Bachelor* and the network is paying.

Regardless of how you were crowned the Big Kahuna of your wedding, now you have complete freedom to host the party of your dreams. All your coin and independent spirit earned you a giant foam middle finger. Anytime your in-laws or family cast doubt or complain, whip it out and wave it in the air. Who's the man now, dog! If they don't like it, they can kiss your financially independent bridal butt.

## Scenario 2:

## Your Family Is Paying for the Wedding

Your parents are thrilled. You're no longer a doomed Jane Austen spinster. A man has extended his hand. A wedding must be planned! Signal the bell tower! Saddle the horses! Alert the chambermaids!

Ah, yes . . . the dowry tradition: giving away daughter = spending cash = shindig. Your proud parents are delivering you into matrimony the Elizabethan way, with bountiful foods, savory wines, and the finest threads. Bravo!

But why is your family the exclusive source of funding four hundred years after the plague? Didn't the in-laws get the memo? Or are they still waiting for a message from the king? Either your family clings to tradition and insists that no one else pays (for honor and for country), or your in-laws tout tradition and prefer to keep their money invested in the NASDAQ rather than the totally awesome wedding band Short Bus.

Milady, don't be offended if your in-laws don't offer to pony up cash. It doesn't (always) mean they disapprove of your union or that they're cheap. They might be respecting the wishes of your old-fashioned family. See, chivalry isn't dead after all.

## Scenario 3:

### Your In-Laws Are Paying for the Wedding

Your in-laws are paying for you to marry their son. Hey, you're way ahead of the curve: they adore you so much, they're making a proper woman out of you. (Someone should.)

Having in-laws who exclusively pay for the wedding is unusual. Extraordinary circumstances must be in play, such as:

- Your parents are in jail or at sea. Either way, they're busy.
- Your family doesn't approve of your "outrageous" union. His family does.
- Your parents are still paying off your William & Mary tuition.
- You sniffed out cash like a police dog at O'Hare and found gold. Digger.
- There are nine girls in your family. No way. No how. No more girls.
- Your in-laws love a good party. They weren't nicknamed "Kegger Kim and Ken" for nothing.

Now that you're tied to your in-laws' coin purse, you're also tied to their whims. They're gunning for steel drums, a nondairy mint cake, and a five-minute swan parade. It's par for the course.

But be mindful: an in-law-funded wedding can drive a wedge between you and your family. So involve your own brood as best you can in the details. If your mother would like to contribute "a little something" to offset the cost of your dress, accept graciously. If there's zero cash flow from your folks' direction, simply because the river is dry, make sure they know that just because they didn't bankroll the party doesn't mean they're not VIPs in your book.

### SCENARIO 4:

### You, Your Family, In-Laws, and Step-In-Laws Are Paying for the Wedding

You're a pinball wizard—and just scored a multiball! With so many relatives ricocheting in all directions with money to burn, you're convinced you'll host the perfect wedding. Wrong. Too many targets with flashing lights. Too many people with opinions. Gutter ball. Game over.

How can you harness the raw animal strength of the multi-headed wedding monster to plan the day of your dreams? Two words: *clarify expectations.* If you're lucky, everyone rips out the same page from *Martha Stewart Weddings* magazine and presents it at your inaugural planning meeting. But if that doesn't happen, how do you blend multiple checkbooks into one event?

- **Get everyone on the same page with a budget.** It's simple. Except when it's not. But if you have "The Number," you can always—ALWAYS—point to it in times of stress. "We're sorry, you guys, but there's just no more room in the budget for life-size cardboard cutouts of your dead relatives. Remember the budget? It hasn't changed. Nor will it."
- **Determine what each family can afford.** Lo and behold, weddings evaporate money. Credit limits are raised. Yes, this is a very important day in your and your in-laws' lives, but there are car payments, rent checks, and grocery bills to tend to the morning after.

- **Designate.** Joint budgets work best when each party has a specific task assigned. Your own parents love to garden, so put them on florist watch. Your in-laws love to dance? They'll enjoy providing the band. There are eleven major pillars to wedding planning: transportation, ceremony location, attire, rings, flowers, catering, music, reception location, cake, photographer, and honeymoon. Match an investor to a cause, and then stick to it.

### "We'll Pay for the Photographer!"

- It's so sweet that your in-laws want to offset wedding costs. However, they routinely neglect phone bills, and last time you saw them, you heard: "Did they shut off the hot water, again? It's only been six months!"
- For overall investment health of the wedding, diversify your assets and avoid junk bonds. Admit it: his folks are a risky venture. They might be enthusiastic overcommitters or just plain bad with money. Either way, it's unnerving.
- To honor their commitment to you, have your partner ask if he can receive payment *before* deadlines. That way, you've got money in the bank and the wedding stays on track. Or offer another, cheaper way for them to contribute to the wedding. A homemade wedding cake? An original poem for the ceremony? Whatever activity you design for spendthrift in-laws, you'll be happier if it doesn't involve plastic promises or rubber checks.

## Third Cousin Angelo

Your guest list is a *Who's Who* list of New Jersey's Italian-American community. Your excited mother-in-law just invited her entire hair salon. Stand firm. Not *all* the waxers need to attend your wedding.

> "There was a 200-person maximum at the wedding hall. My in-laws submitted 140 names. Obviously, the e-mails and conversations we had been having for three months were forgotten. Yes, my in-laws are very social people. That's not my problem. I handed the phone to my fiancé and took a bath."
>
> AMANDA, PHILADELPHIA

Managing the guest list takes the skill of a master negotiator. As the president, founder, and CEO of your wedding, you must give your employees explicit parameters—the head count is nonnegotiable. Of course, some lucky brides will have in-laws that invite only four people, one of whom is the groom. That's

### In-Laws, RSVPs, and the Postal System

Apparently, cousin-in-law Susan *is* attending the wedding (so your in-laws claim). Well, there's no proof. You haven't received her RSVP card. People! Is it that difficult to put the thing in the mail? It's pre-stamped! You won't believe it until you see it.

And then there's cousin-in-law Larry, who mailed his RSVP card so quickly he didn't write his name on it. Here's a trick for these in-laws (and undoubtedly some of your beloved relatives as well): before you send out invitations, use pencil and lightly write a number corresponding to their name on your guest list, on the back side of the reply card. This way "The Mysterious Case of the Anonymous Wedding Guest" is closed, Perry Mason–style.

a *different* problem. For the rest, your in-laws will use the following techniques from the "how to guilt the sweet bride into higher numbers" book. Oh, you didn't think they *had* that book? Girl, they all do.

### The Damned Plus-Ones

Single people of the world, you're fabulous. We love you. Sometimes, we want to be you. And we hope all of you get married one day, so we can laugh as you go through the hell we're going through now. (Did I say hell? I meant happiness. I get those H-words confused sometimes.)

But now you're a thorn in our side with your ambiguous plus-one status. Rule of thumb: guests that have been dating for more than six months have the right to a plus-one. The "totally hunky" man named Leon that your fiancé's Aunt Penny met two weeks ago on a cruise to Aruba does not get an invite.

> "You always wanted to invite your old favorite baby-sitter to your wedding. You didn't realize she'd be coming with your father-in-law! Weird, right?"
>
> JESSICA, SAN DIEGO

Just remember, a wedding is not an event for awkward blind dates just because your cousin-in-law doesn't want to come alone. It is an opportunity for awkward sex between this cousin and your college friend after a half-dozen glasses of champagne.

### Buying the Guest List

Your in-laws are Mr. and Mrs. Daddy Warbucks. Great. Now they want to pay more in return for a bigger head count. Every member of "the club" must attend, including the groundskeeper. On the bright side, these guests would easily complete your china registry and leave you with enough credit that you'll never touch a paper plate again. The downside is walking down the aisle and hearing people whisper, "Who is *that*? Is that the bride?"

A wise American poet once said, "Mo' money, mo' problems." And frankly, you can't be bought. Toss the Dom Perignon overboard and hold on to your dreams. Otherwise it's going to end up feeling as if you're invited to their wedding, and not the other way around. Redirect your in-laws' enthusiasm and bank account toward an extravagant engagement party at Lake Como. Oh, you poor little rich girl, the possibilities are endless. Can we move on now?

### Live-at-Home Losers

Barry, age forty, still lives at home with his parents, who also happen to be dear friends of your in-laws. You've heard his name mentioned before. You've heard about his outrageous pay-per-view bills. You know all about his psoriasis. But that doesn't buy him a ticket to your celebration. Sometimes an adult child is better left uninvited. (Presumably he can spend one evening unsupervised.) For all you know, you could be inviting the Sasquatch. It's a no go. And Barry will thank you for the night alone with Howard Stern, the TV remote, and the vibrating bed.

### Distant Cousins

Who *are* these people? Most Americans were immigrants. Most are proud of their heritage and their family trees. But not everyone from five-generations-ago Iran needs to attend your wedding. It's a nice sentiment, but it's not up to you to secure travel arrangements from a small village 200 miles outside Tehran to

New York for "family members" that your fiancé has never met. A little pruning of the family tree is good for everyone, because really, you have enough on your plate.

### Your Wedding the Eighth-Grade Dance

Remind your in-laws that your wedding isn't a popularity contest. Tell them that they have plenty of friends and ratcheting up their guest list from 25 to 250 won't make them more popular. Identify the extra fat: the guests that don't fit in with the others. There are two explanations for the appearance of these names: either your in-laws hope to gain something from the invite or they're using your wedding as payback.

By inviting the chief of police, your father-in-law hopes that he'll overlook the out-of-date liquor license at the family restaurant. By inviting the neighbors, he's hoping they'll forget about the lawn mower he borrowed eight years ago. Conversely, certain names are missing from the guest list. Strangely, your aunt-in-law's name has been omitted. Her husband is invited. Her kids are invited. This isn't an oversight. This was purposeful. A line was drawn in the sand last summer when she drove off and left your mother-in-law stranded in the dressing room at Fashion Bug. Welcome to the vendetta guest list.

Also, if unacceptable guests like your fiancé's psychotic ex-lover, your father-in-law's illegitimate daughter, or Gary Busey pop up on the list, you do have some say. Make a stink. Give 'em hell. Threaten to boycott. On the other hand, if harmless (albeit strange) invitees like Susan, the tech assistant who helped with your in-law's recent colonoscopy, are within your in-laws' head count quota, grin and bear it.

### Witness Protection Program

When planning a wedding, sometimes it's best to be incognito. It's not always safe to give in-laws your e-mail address, work number, and daily schedule. You can't be at the constant beck and call of your in-laws, and their breaking news regarding the sushi table. You've got a little thing called a "job" and a "boss" and those pesky "deadlines."

If you elect to talk on the phone, which is a more polite but less time-efficient modus operandi, use caller ID and pre-planned times to talk to your in-laws. If you randomly dial them, inevitably your step-father-in-law can't find his hearing aid or his dog is barking, and you'll just have to say it again. And this time, louder.

## The In-Law Bridal Party

It's like college admissions. There are those who are accepted because they deserve it, and those who get in because of legacy. Unlike Yale, you draw the line. Don't feel pressured to include your sweetie's sister (the one who ran away to Thailand last summer and returned with a large angel tattoo that no Vera Wang dress will hide) because of her birthright. She won't care. She has more important things to worry about, like hepatitis C test results.

> "I felt pressure to include my sister-in-law in the bridal party. She is a model. Eventually, my priest had to pull her aside. She was strutting down the aisle like it was fashion week and acting a little too seductive. I'm glad he said something. Can you imagine?"
>
> ALYSSA, NASHUA

Here's a good rule of thumb: include your own family, close friends who selflessly moved you into fourth-floor walk-up apartments, and siblings-in-law you trust and like. Try to keep it under six bridesmaids and six groomsmen. We know your Catholic in-laws birthed nine kids. Now you're forced to use restraint where they didn't.

> "My husband had 12 groomsmen because our families are so large. It was ridiculous—it became a frat party. Any time you have that many men hanging out together in a stuffy environment, they rebel and do crass things. At the ceremony, the last guy couldn't even fit, so he was standing out the door."
>
> ELISE, ASHEVILLE

## Revelation of Family Secrets

Before planning the seating chart, you didn't know that Uncle Marty couldn't sit within a 15-foot radius of Larry Conway. Apparently, they had a blowout fight over a salted pretzel during a layover at La Guardia Airport ten years ago and now their restraining order is your problem.

Don't think that you'll get to know your husband's extended family at the wedding. You probably won't even talk to them. But fear not—you'll learn plenty about their likes, dislikes, and who they've pissed off while planning the seating chart.

### To Place or Not to Place Cards

That is the question. Oh, it's a royal pain to alphabetize your guests and draw a table diagram for the reception hall. However, table cards *and* place cards set a lovely tone. Forcing your families to mingle can be as fun as dropping Mentos into a liter of Diet Coke. There's so much excitement, possibility, and anticipation!

> "There were endless e-mails about the seating chart for our two families. We wanted to blend the groups together. My family is from California; my in-laws are from Virginia. At the last minute, my mother-in-law submitted her list and everyone from her family was seated at the same tables. And worse, they had the best seats in the house."
>
> ERICA, LOUISVILLE

### Grade-A Choice Meat

Yes, there are good seats and bad seats at a wedding. From your in-laws' throne, they want an unobstructed view of the dance floor and nothing less for their friends and family.

But *someone* has to sit near the exit. It's a fact of life. Accept that some guests will be baffled. Accept that your in-laws will be miffed. And know that you will hardly notice any of this on the day of your wedding. Unless a centerpiece catches fire, in which case the people seated near the fire exits will be thrilled.

> "My father-in-law approached the wedding planner because one guest (from his side of the family) was so upset about where she was sitting that she wanted to leave. The guest thought her seat obviously represented the new 'pecking order' of the family, and she didn't like it."
>
> LIZ, ATLANTA

Be conscious that not all of your in-laws' family and friends are seated in the dark corners of the restaurant, hall, or backyard. Sprinkle your guests near the kitchen and bathrooms, too. So bride-to-be, how do you deal with inevitable seating battles?

- Deputize a friend or relative to deal exclusively with seating issues. When a problem arises, they'll unleash the PR spin on your behalf. Be smart; pick a spokesperson with the gift of gab. Think Kelly Ripa.
- There are two tiers of seating commitments: first, it's table or escort cards; and second, it's place cards. At the very least, the "etiquette gods" demand table cards. But your in-laws insist on place cards for each guest. So, let your in-laws determine who is "well suited" to talk to one another. You take a nap.
- When Ms. Misery or her husband corners you in the bathroom stall to complain about their seats, placate them with the following statement: "It's such a gorgeous reception hall. I'm so thrilled to celebrate with you! Thanks for saying hi." Then flee the bathroom, even if you can't flush first. Mission accomplished: do not engage with a crazy person.

Remember, after all that fuss and planning, your guests will take it upon themselves to switch place cards. And frighteningly enough, your in-laws might do the same thing.

> "During the cocktail hour of my wedding reception, my mother-in-law sneaked into the hall and switched place card arrangements at the tables. This is after I had decided the plan. It was her way of ensuring that her friends and family had the best seats. I complimented her on her determination. What a lunatic!"
>
> MIA, SAN ANTONIO

### The Capulets and the Montagues

Table and/or place cards are essential if you have feuding families. In this day and age, people just can't get along. You'd be naive to expect everyone to simply put aside their gripes just because you decided to get married—do you *remember* your bat mitzvah?

Your mother-in-law used to have a best friend. Then one day she returned home and found her friend in bed with her husband. For the love of God, seat these ladies far, far apart so that no one launches the sea bass. Especially not at 80 bucks a plate.

### The In-Law Hosted Bridal Shower

You are being celebrated, bride! You're being "showered" with attention and presents! Why aren't you happy? Is your stepmother-in-law dominating your social calendar? Is this supposed "gift of a bridal shower" actually just a ploy to tie up your phone line? Why are you being asked about every detail?

"I had four bridal showers, three of which were hosted by in-laws and step-in-laws. This took up so much time of my time! Why so many? Not everyone was invited to each. Certain people didn't make the A-list. I couldn't say no because a bridal shower is 'a gift' and I wanted to be gracious and appreciative."

ABBY, CHICAGO

Exhale. Inhale. It's hard not to feel overwhelmed. Resist internalizing the anxiety of in-law wedding demands, so as not to trigger your bowels at the shower. You don't want the ladies crowding into the bathroom to watch you unwrap a Crate and Barrel rolling pin.

In-law-hosted bridal showers often result in one thing: an overwhelming amount of loot. Don't feel guilty. Like the Latter-Day Saints, you have spent a year on a mission to involve your in-laws in your new life. After such a feat, you deserve the cinnamon-colored KitchenAid blender. It's a medal of appreciation, and a giant token of in-law expectation that you will blend healthy smoothies for their darling boy every morning of your lives together.

"My wedding weekend began with a private ceremony in a park. My in-laws are divorced and bitterly hate each other. My mother-in-law was walking down the aisle for my ceremony and tripped on a few loose rocks. She nearly fell over. My father-in-law smirked, not offering a hand. At the last moment, my cousin shot out an arm to help her. My father-in-law would rather she fell flat on her face."

NICOLE, SCOTTSDALE

The wedding table is *your* turf. At the end of the cocktail hour, amid the stampede to the reception hall, you've ensured that mortal enemies end up at separate tables and keep the in-law drama to a minimum. Pray the conga line stays peaceful and the break-dancing battle remains calm. This is *the* reason for wedding-inspired headbands and knee pads. In case you didn't already know.

### Wedding Invitations

You selected an ivory William Arthur note card. You chose thermography and embellished the invitations with a gold and green leaf. You purchased hundreds of Breast Cancer Awareness stamps. You think—people are going to *love* these invites! Well, after it's slammed into a desk drawer and filed away for later use, here's how your in-law family interprets your wedding invitation (if they didn't already misplace it):

*Sarah Spoke* (*not the other girlfriend we liked more*)

*and Justin England*

(*They're not paying for this thing. Since when do their names go first?!*)

*warmly invite you to celebrate in their marriage*

(*I'm getting old*)

*on Saturday, the twentieth of September*

(*Whatever happened to June brides? June is a lovely time of the year.*)

*at half past five in the evening*

(*Just great. We have to worry about parking overnight.*)

*Villard Vineyards*

(*They're not getting married in a church? My son agreed to this? They're going to hell.*)

*Napa Valley, California*

(*Maybe I'll like my daughter-in-law more with unlimited pinot noir.*)

*Adults only*

(*It's so obvious that she hates children. The writing is on the wall.*)

*Attire is semi-formal*

(*"This is too formal" or "This isn't formal enough." People will look ridiculous in the photos. What a piss-poor decision.*)

*Please RSVP by the fifteenth of August*

(*They know we're going—no need to tell them.*)

Wording on wedding invitations is as important as wording on a gravestone. For eternity, the world will know who had the honor of paying for the wedding. Everyone wants top billing! To be on the marquee! To have the spotlight!

This is tricky business. If you and your sweetie, your own divorced parents, and your divorced in-laws are collectively footing the bill, the age-old proper tradition is still to list the parents of the bride as the hosts. But when in doubt:

- You can always throw tradition around like a battle-ax when there are multiple investors in the wedding. Remember, you and yours are the executive producers of the show. So be modern and place your names atop. If guests want to mingle after the party ends and examine the credits—fine, let them. Who cares then anyway? Show's over!
- Conversely, if your in-laws are footing the bill but are too embarrassed to take top billing on the invitation for reasons ranging from: a) they don't want the friends who aren't invited to know they're hosting; b) they think your shindig will be half-assed and they want no credit for it; or c) they can't possibly decide anything, ever, just thank them for their check and move on.
- Finally, when making decisions that affect all families at once, get things in writing. Prevent revisionist history. Encourage all parties to voice their opinion via e-mail. So when they change their minds—again—two hours before the printer finishes your invitation, show your in-laws their own words, dated October 12: "Please place your names atop the invitation. We love that idea!"

### Dropping the Bomb

Your mother-in-law's childhood friend can't make the wedding. The photographer isn't taking table portraits at the reception. Your own mother is changing the color of her dress. Whatever the news that will flip your in-laws' lid, tell them via e-mail. A colon, a hyphen, and a close parenthesis typed in succession will make the e-mail much nicer. Actually, it won't. You know what would? Writing a nicer e-mail.

## The Busy Bee

Arranging tampons in the restroom baskets, knotting strings on programs, or cat-sitting during the honeymoon are perfect tasks for the buzzing in-law who wants to be included. She's the needy girl in high school who desperately wants to brush your hair. Throw her a bone. So you're prepared, there are five wedding tasks your mother-in-law wants to do.

### 1. Wedding Dress Shopping

Your mother-in-law wants be one of the girls! When looking for a wedding dress, you undergo a lot of self-discovery and, let's face it, self-criticism. You need someone to support you when the Slovakian wedding dress consultant tells you that you're short-waisted and flat-chested. Will your mother-in-law have your back? Or will she capitalize on the moment and steer you toward the V-waistline that exponentially expands your ass? Here are truths about opening up your heart and dressing room to your in-law.

**TRUTH : YOUR IN-LAW WILL BE DISTRACTING.**

It's not like she's spinning plates while singing *Tosca*. Her mode of distraction is much more subtle. And you need to "focus-people-focus!" to find a stylish dress that fits the bill. Bonding with your in-law may distract you from honing in on beadwork. You're about to drop some benjamins. Pay attention! *Achtung!*

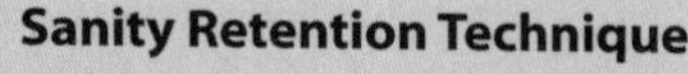

### Sanity Retention Technique

Don't publicly announce each time you go dress shopping. Sometimes a girl needs to be alone with her taffeta and veil. Okay?

**TRUTH: YOUR IN-LAW WILL SEE YOU TOPLESS AND IN A THONG.**

The cellulite. The backne. The in-between bikini waxing. It's all there for the world to see. Your in-law needs to help you climb into dresses, lace corsets, and slip on heels, while the seamstress lifts your skirt and top for measurements. It's *your* grill. Protect it.

### Sanity Retention Technique

If you're timid with your tatas or humble with your hootie, plan your shaving regime accordingly and wear panties that fall under the category of "full coverage."

**TRUTH: YOUR IN-LAW WILL JUDGE YOU.**

It's human nature to pass harsh judgments on fashion. Your wedding dress says it all: the past, present, and future with her son. Your in-law is only connecting the dots.

| | |
|---|---|
| *If the dress is short:* | You're a slut and will probably sleep with a windsurfing instructor on your honeymoon if you aren't sleeping with one already. |
| *If the dress is ornate:* | You're as high maintenance as a B-level celebrity at Fashion Week and her son should find solace in the arms of his simple-minded secretary. |
| *If the dress is plain:* | You're boring and her son's only excitement in life will be watching *Wheel of Fortune* every night in a beige living room. |
| *If the dress is expensive:* | You're a financial floozy and will piss away paychecks on hair highlights and purses with nothing left to feed her starving son and grandchildren. |
| *If the dress is untraditional:* | You will poison her grandchildren with your artsyness. |

**Sanity Retention Technique**

Read her body language and send a few messages of your own. If she grimaces because she thinks it's "too much cleavage," tell yourself: "I've still got it!" Then show her how you can hide your lipstick in those girls. It's your dress, your boobs, and your lipstick.

**TRUTH: YOUR IN-LAW HAS NO TASTE.**

You just want the facts, ma'am. Does this shade of white draw blood from your face? Is the tiara too much? Do you look like Little Bo Peep? Your immediate family who share your coloring, or your best friends who share your taste, will tell it to you straight.

> **Sanity Retention Technique**
>
> Be wary if you sense that your mother-in-law or sister-in-law wants to look better than you at the wedding. Don't fall for their ploy: "Here's another dress in stark white to check out . . ." Call in reinforcements: Whisper to the clerk that you don't want to see anything in that shade, "so as not to waste her time."

## 2. The Wedding Favor

Your mother-in-law is as energetic as a chipmunk and brimming with ideas. Excitedly, she phones to tell you the story about how she spotted the perfect wedding favors. "They're so you!" That's why she went ahead and ordered them. So heads up, bride, a hundred and fifty tiny porcelain unicorns will arrive on your doorstep next week: "Isn't that wonderful?"

> "My mother-in-law thought it was a great idea to buy 300 phone cards as wedding favors. We had relatives visiting from China and she believed they would love to call internationally for free. Unfortunately, my idea of an elegant table setting did not include AT&T calling cards. Luckily, one week before the wedding the calling cards expired. But at the last minute, my mother-in-law still managed to sprinkle 300 Nescafé packets on the table. She thought guests would love the free coffee."
>
> June, Washington, D.C.

What to do? Stop questioning why your mother-in-law wants to be so involved. She just does. Yes, it's annoying, but it's (kind of) helpful—*do you really want to spend hours finding wedding favors?* Instead of focusing on her questionable taste, give her explicit directions to:

1. Cancel nonapproved existing orders.
2. Study the photos of adorable favors you give her.
3. Open the Internet link you send her and purchase *those* favors.

If your in-law hems and haws that she didn't discover the favors on her own, remind her gently that it's your day and that she's helping to make it perfect. If she exorcises her creative demons and creates jellybean magnets bearing your names, hide them in a hip paper bag, mug, or silk pouch. She had good intentions; she just got carried away with the glue gun.

## 3. The Friendly Donation

Curiously, your mother-in-law has stockpiled hundreds of frozen miniature shrimp quiches left over from her tenure as social chair to the Junior Women's League of Philadelphia. Now she wants to donate these shrimp-flavored petri dishes to your special day.

Fearful that your wedding will show up on the 10 o'clock news as "Killer Quiche Attacks!" you inform her that the caterer charges extra to serve food that is not his own and it would actually *cost money* to use her donated shrimp tarts.

If she's upset, calm her by promising to use the quiches at upcoming holidays. They'll be served alongside the hundreds of frozen Samoa Girl Scout cookies you discovered in her basement the other day.

If your in-law generously donates the time and food of others, like getting her "handicapable" newspaper boy to be your photographer—for free!—kindly say no thank you. Be strong, because this "generous spirit" will live long after the wedding day.

## 4. The Location Scout

There's nothing like a hefty location fee or an iron-clad contract that brings out the worry wart in us all. To assuage your fears, your in-law volunteers to visit the location with you. Suddenly the only sound she can make is the clearing of her throat. It's her cute way of disapproving. Either your mother-in-law ate a box of saltines and a tub of peanut butter before your meeting, or she's a classic harrumpher.

> **har-rumph** [huh-ruhmf]
> 1. To clear the throat audibly in a self-important manner: *The professor harrumphed at his students.* 2. To express oneself gruffly: *She harrumphed for a while over the proposal.*

You can join the passive-aggressive party and ask if she'd like a glass of water. Otherwise, just relax. All wedding locations ultimately degenerate into a place where guests cut a rug to the "chicken dance." And if she remains speechless, here's a chart you can use to interpret those harrumphs at every turn:

| Wedding Location | What You Think | What Your In-Law Thinks |
|---|---|---|
| Your parents' backyard | "I remember when I was five running through the yard with my dog, Rex." | "The septic system won't hold. By 7 PM, we'll be dancing in a swamp of toilet water. |
| Your in-laws' backyard | "I've always admired their gazebo. I wonder if they'll finally let me sit in it." | "What a mooch." |
| The Italian restaurant, Gino's on the Sound | "Tuscan Chianti, cremini mushroom risotto, pesto Parmesan twists—it will be a gastronomical feast." | "Wasn't Gino's the Clam Shack a few years ago? Didn't the Department of Health shut it down?" |

| Wedding Location | What You Think | What Your In-Law Thinks |
| --- | --- | --- |
| The 300-person Grand Ballroom at Miami Marriott Biscayne Bay | "P-Diddy and J-Lo hosted New Year's bashes here. Cool." | "I'm glad her parents are footing the bill for this circus." |
| A Vermont mountaintop | "The view is breathtaking!" | "*Vermont?* I hate hippies! How can she do this to us?" |
| The historic Marble House mansion in Newport, R.I. | "The architecture, the style, and the view of the ocean are so Jackie O." | "Isn't that the mansion where so-and-so threw herself off a cliff the night before her wedding?" |
| A 150-foot party yacht | "Big Pimpin'!" | "Hello—*barf bags*? And didn't she see *Titanic*? Such a tragedy." |
| The St. Paul's Church Reception Hall | "They'll be so happy that I kept cost down. One location and no fee!" | "She's a religious freak. I hope there's wine." |
| The Contemporary Art Museum | I can't believe I'm marrying before Rothko's *Orange and Yellow, 1956*. | "Anything post-Renoir is worthless." |
| Philadelphia's Botanical Gardens | "Gorgeous roses, lily ponds, and swans are a picture-perfect backdrop to 'I do.'" | "Doesn't she read the papers? Wild mute swans are carriers of the H5N1 virus." |
| The Lodge at Molokai, Hawaii | "My wedding will be like a long honeymoon with my closest friends and family." | "Now everyone I've ever known will see me in a bathing suit." |

## 5. The Homemade Present: Something Blue

This is the worst kind of wedding gift: "Look at me, world! I took hours to make! If I'm not worn or displayed at the wedding, my son and daughter-in-law don't love me." This gift was made by and for your in-law, with little consideration for you.

Your talented Jewish mother-in-law knit a surprise blue yarmulke for your fiancé three days before the wedding. Unfortunately, you and your fiancé already agreed that he wasn't wearing one at your Hindu-Jewish interfaith ceremony.

Don't feel bad. She could have spent her time more wisely: helping the poor, recycling plastic bottles, and not applying eleventh-hour pressure on your religious decisions. Suggest that your father-in-law wear the yarmulke. Now its public debut is on someone else's head, while also color-coordinating with his eyes. See, it all works out.

## The Rehearsal Dinner

Traditionally hosted by the groom's parents, this event is *the* opportunity for your in-laws to leave an uncensored mark on the wedding. If your in-laws felt shut out of the wedding process, they will view this as their chance to be seen and heard. "Ladies and Gentlemen, please rise to greet . . . the groom's parents! The unsung heroes of the wedding! The people with *real* taste!" You get the point.

How can you avoid letting this dinner become your Last In-Law Supper? Treat your in-laws like free-range chickens. They can run around like maniacs all they want, inside a penned area you create. There are no: Bird of Paradise flowers! Baseball-themed tables! Or mechanical bulls! in their pen. Whatever their style and unrealized desires, try to keep it in balance with your big day. Parity is key.

### Problem: Your In-Laws Want to Show Off Serious Bling for the Rehearsal Dinner. You Wish They Wouldn't.

**Solution:** Afraid your in-laws' dinner party will overshadow the wedding? Your fears are probably valid—they did hire Jay *Z*'s party planner. Urge your partner to speak with his parents, since they aren't listening to you and don't share your dream of a "low-key, understated wedding." Simply say: "We enjoy your exuberance and support, but let's pump your mad money and chips into the headline event, instead of the kick-off party."

Trade your single rose bouquet for EXTREMELY rare Thai orchids. Or print self-designed, simple escort cards on outlandishly expensive paper. If your in-laws still want credit for the event (and attention for all the bling), make a note in your program: "Flowers, filet mignon, and '82 Cabernet hand-selected by Big Pappa- and Mamma-in-Law."

### Problem: Your In-Laws Want to Host the Rehearsal Dinner at Al's Bar, Complete with Pistachios, Peanuts, and Miller Lite.

**Solution:** You obviously had something else in mind. You didn't buy that gorgeous Catherine Malandrino black number to prance around in a dive bar. Nor did you work on that glowing wedding-day complexion to display it in gritty pub lighting.

It doesn't take money to class-up an event. It takes taste, and sometimes your in-laws' style barometer is off (case in point: the eagle bandannas they wear every day). Work within their budget and shoot for a venue at least half a step up from Al's. Not so chi-chi that you lose your in-laws' "unique" vision for the rehearsal dinner, but no sawdust on the floor, either. Bar food and homemade moonshine can be made almost elegant with the right location, lighting, and soundtrack. At sunset, overlooking the lake, with a few well-placed flowers, no one cares that they're eating fried buffalo wings.

### Problem: Your In-Laws Want to Engage in Their Own Religious Traditions (On Your Behalf of Course).

**Solution:** So his parents are disappointed that you're not having a proper Catholic wedding. When the lights dim, the audience quiets, and the rehearsal dinner curtains lift, your in-laws want to pray. You know what? Let 'em. Provided their religious beliefs don't involve live snakes, let them stand on a pulpit provided by

Mamma Rosa's Ristorante and bless you, the wine, and the food—*for just a few minutes.* Don't worry about it; it's their moment to tell everyone that they're praying (and paying) for us all. Hey, at least they're getting it out of their system now, before the main event.

## Toasts: Give the Drunk Guy a Microphone

Traditionally, the clinking of glasses was said to be a way to frighten off evil spirits, but nowadays toasts frighten guests all on their own. You're generally prepared for what your own family might say, or at least capable of threatening them effectively to keep things clean. But your in-laws still have a few tricks up their collective sleeve:

| Types of In-Law Toasters | The Damage They Cause |
|---|---|
|   | "My husband's brother started off so well with, "I knew this girl was special," and then he continued, 'because normally when Dan went to the Jersey shore with us, he would bang every girl in sight. But he was content to just bang her every weekend. That's how we all knew she was the one.'" DANIELLE, PRINCETON |
|   | "I thought it would be nice to let my father-in-law speak, but he spoke for 37 minutes! At 17 minutes in, the banquet manager ran out and asked: 'Where are we?' I answered that we're out of the bassinet and onto age 7. I signaled for the band to play when he moved onto the college years. It was ridiculous." CAROL, BOULDER |

"My sister-in-law gave a PowerPoint slide show for her toast. There were multiple-choice questions that guests had to yell out answers to. She loves being the center of attention. Her toast got huge laughs—especially when a photo of my fiancé passed out in a tub flashed onscreen. You know, it's my wedding day and I don't want the love of my life looking like an ass."

AMELIA, TULSA

"My sister-in-law's boyfriend grabbed the microphone mid-party. He said that I looked pretty. Then he mentioned a night at Señor Frog's when we did shots together and how that was fun. The DJ started playing over him. It was so awkward."

ELIZABETH, ASPEN

"My brother-in-law was drunk and said that I groveled to get the ring and hung around until Mike finally gave in. He said I was like a hungry dog waiting for the ring. I've never forgiven him."

SARAH, TAMPA

"My sister-in-law was such a basket case when it came time for her to talk that she checked her note cards for every word and mispronounced my name!"

ALTHEA, BATON ROUGE

## Wedding Ceremonies

YOUR IN-LAWS: "Do you take Father Nikos to be your wedding officiant?"

YOU: "No."

YOUR IN-LAWS: "But he's known Billy since he was three."

YOU: "Father Nikos is estranged from his family and was nearly kicked out of the church for listing his ceremonial robe on eBay."

YOUR IN-LAWS: "That was just hearsay."

When our Founding Father Thomas Jefferson penned the Declaration of Independence, proclaiming our right to pursue life, liberty, and happiness, he obviously wasn't thinking about your wedding ceremony. Your Polish, Jainist, Italian, Muslim in-laws want it their way or the proverbial highway to hell.

Your in-laws want to see themselves in your ceremony. They want their Russian Orthodox priest, not your family's Russian Orthodox priest, to perform the wedding. Their fear, of course, is that when you're married, their son will spend all the holidays with your family, and only visit them on Columbus Day for a few hours, if they're lucky.

Oh, how they lament that their traditions will be lost in your future home—you-threatening-young-bride-you—and worse, that their grandkids will not be practicing Zoroastrians or Lutherans or Seventh-Day Adventists.

The bottom line is: you and your fiancé must decide what is important for the two of you, and only then consider what's meaningful to your families. For centuries, couples have married from different backgrounds and have been able to blend them successfully, enriching not only their lives but also the lives of their in-laws. Look at the Hapsburgs. The Medicis. French kings. English queens—more political success was achieved by marriage than by means of war. Snap!

> "My husband and I decided to include his Filipino tradition of releasing a pair of doves into the air during our ceremony. As I joyfully raised my arms and the doves soared into the air, my strapless gown loosened and I released my own pair of doves to my guests."
>
> LISA, HONOLULU

Martin Luther King Jr. said, "We may have all come on different ships, but we are in the same boat now." Despite these encouraging words from Dr. King, your in-laws could surprise you one week, one day, or one hour before your wedding with any of these ancient traditions.

- Your Croatian mother-in-law hopes to replace your veil with a scarf and cover your wedding dress with an apron after the ceremony.
- *"You're drinking tea, sharing sugared sweets, and taking Communion—right?"*
- Your brother-in-law just had a truckload of lumber delivered. He's assembling your canopy, huppah, or mandap right now.
- *"I hope you're wearing jade, 24-karat gold, or changing into a red dress."*
- Your African-American in-laws ready themselves to "jump the broom."
- *"I found this great passage to read aloud from the Sura al-Fatiha."*
- Your Persian uncle-in-law sets up for the "knife dance."
- Your Shinto-practicing grandfather-in-law wants to know if you're using "the purification wand."

When life throws you a curveball, you learn how to hit curveballs. The force is strong in you, young Jedi. Be not afraid to make waves.

Stand tall when you excitedly enter the ornate cathedral for your ceremony and your Quaker in-laws cringe. Don't be fazed when your Japanese in-laws are horrified that you're not performing the *haraigushi* (the honoring of family ritual). Walk

**The Pea under the Mattress: Prenuptial Agreements**

Your in-laws want to pee a circle around their property. They adore the house in Reno and want to ensure that it "stays in the family." And heavens to Betsy if the amethyst bracelet from 1822 falls into "the wrong hands."

> "My in-laws sprung the pre-nup one week before the big day. It sent me into a tailspin—mostly because the pre-nup had a clause that said that if I remarried within five years of the death of my spouse, I would lose everything. Hey, if you're dead, you're dead! I should have seen this coming. My in-laws are lawyers and my husband's first wife cleaned them out."
>
> PAMELA, LAS VEGAS

Sure, you can shrug it off; however, pre-nups can rattle the calmest of souls. Part of you protests and part of you is fine signing the dotted line. Rest assured; no one is whispering the word *divorce* under their breath. They're saying it out loud.

Ultimately, the decision is between you and your partner. Pre-nups are always subject to negotiation. After all, your honey didn't marry you to be his "yes man," did he?!

right up to your Italian in-laws and tell them you're not carrying around a coin purse, no matter what they say.

Not everyone is going to be 100 percent happy all the time. Welcome to life. *Namaste*. And may the circling of the sacred fires during your wedding ceremony be the only fiery pit that you encounter in life. *MaSalaama*. Amen.

## Remember, It Could Always Be Worse

Okay, so maybe your in-law family is clueless! Annoying! Too distant! Or meddling! But at the very least, they love you (somewhere deep inside). The worst story by far is the in-law family that attends your wedding simply to spite you:

> "Perhaps, my in-laws believed in the philosophy—if you ignore it, it will go away. This is incredibly painful, but my in-laws ignored me the entire day of my wedding. They didn't utter a word in my direction. Sure, they posed for photographs. They even cracked a smile. But they *never* once said anything directly to me. It was horrible. Of course I was in tears for a few moments in the bathroom with my sister during the reception. If you think your in-laws are going to do this—don't let them attend. It's as simple as that. I'm happy to report that I'm happily married with a baby! So, we didn't let them stop us!"
>
> SHARON, BOSTON

Now didn't that little dose of schadenfreude work wonders? Stay calm. Remain focused—it's only a few more weeks that you have to upkeep manicured nails. Enjoy seeing your name printed on cocktail napkins and participating in lengthy discussions about what makes a great party "mix." Revel in knowing that people traveled far and wide to see you in a pretty dress, because when the honeymoon ends, the next chapter—the never-ending-thank-you-note-writing phase—begins.

# sharing your bundle of joy

**Babies are *so* adorable. Grandparents-in-law, less so.**

EXCERPT FROM THE AUTHOR'S DIARY:

> *At first being pregnant was a wonderful bonding experience with my mother-in-law. It's the one thing I've ever done that she openly praises. Initially, I was overwhelmed with her love, support, and help. But now she's overwhelming me with oversharing. I'm six months pregnant, and I've learned more about her own pregnancy constipation, hemorrhoids, soda-cracker diet, insomnia, and butt acne than I want to know. And now that I'm shaped like a hippo and peeing every five seconds, I'm her perfect captive audience. She stops by with groceries and stays to tell me how many stitches it took to patch up her episiotomy. If I weren't pregnant, I wouldn't have to hear this! I could throw a rope out the window, rappel down the side of the building, and make my escape through the city sewers.*

## Baby-Makers Step Up

Whether you've been trying for years or you sneezed while ovulating, now you're knocked up. The second, third, and fourth pregnancy tests all show the same blue line and say the same thing. In the blink of an eye, you're going to be a mom, to which you immediately respond: "Crap. Twins run in his family."

Eventually you calm down and, in the sweetest way possible, tell your significant other. Of course, he has his own thoughts: "Crap. Twins run in my family."

Then he calms down. He stops thinking about his bike FOR ONE SECOND and starts to ponder life as a dad. But then his thoughts predictably drift back to his bike. Only now he's thinking about baby bike helmets.

Let's skip the part when the two of you rejoice, panic, and Photoshop your faces together to discover what your offspring will look like—this never works and only makes you more nervous about Baby inheriting his nose with your recessive chin.

Just as you two are getting used to the idea that you're now a threesome, you need to figure out when to tell your in-laws about the little person growing in your belly. Will it be moments before your walk down the aisle for your wedding ceremony? Or will it be when you can no longer handle them criticizing you for "beefing up"?

> "I had to tell my in-laws that I was pregnant; we were visiting them. My mother-in-law and stepfather-in-law promised they wouldn't tell anyone, because I was only 8 weeks along. They live in a small town in southern Kentucky, where everyone knows everyone, and I didn't want to be 'the girl who had a miscarriage' because I am already 'the girl from Massachusetts.' The next morning after breakfast,

my husband and I went to rent a bike. As soon as I rang the service bell, the clerk jumped the counter and hugged me. He wanted to know if it's a boy. So much for privacy."

SUSAN, BOSTON

Your in-laws are immediately aware when "their" sperm scored a touchdown with the egg in your body. They rise in the middle of the night, sensing a disturbance in the force. Knowing they're a grandparent, aunt, or uncle is thrilling, but at the same time it makes them feel old. This explains your in-law family's sudden hysteria to be healthy and take life by the balls! After all, they want to witness every milestone in your baby's life. So thanks for inspiring them to get that goiter checked! Thanks for inspiring them to run a marathon! You're the best!

As the brood mare, you've anchored your relationship in the family. With this child, you and your in-laws are irrefutably linked—*forever*. That's why your in-laws are suddenly so nice; they're buttering you up to gain unimpeded access to your uterus.

Grandchildren can make in-laws loopy. And whatever relationship you had with them before is suddenly subject to renegotiation. There are three stages of dealing with in-laws when you're creating life, each with its perks and pressures: the pregnancy stage, the birth and newborn stage, and the beyond stage. If you don't like one phase, just wait. In a few short months, it changes. Ah, the beauty of young motherhood . . .

## Pregnancy

For nine months, it's a crash course in how to deal with unsolicited advice. If you get the chance, grow some thicker skin in addition to the baby in your belly. You'll need it.

### Spilling the Beans

It starts off small. You quietly whisper the baby news to your mom and dad. They sing, dance, rip off their clothes, and fly! Their joy snowballs and you're addicted to spreading the Word. So, you tell friends over tapas. They hurl themselves off their stools in joy, all the while toasting you with sangria you can't drink! Who cares! The spotlight feels warm and wonderful.

Before you know it, you share the news with the heavyset lady sitting next to you on the subway. She smiles broadly and spins wildly around the subway pole. Everyone is so happy for you! Finally, you tell your in-laws. It's unclear how they found out that "everyone else knew before them" and they're furious that they were "the last to know."

Ultimately, it's your choice when and with whom you share your news. If you want to build goodwill with your in-laws, try to include them in the inner circle along with your parents and closest friends. Prepare to say something like: "As soon as we hung up with my Ob-Gyn, we called you guys!" or "We just found out ourselves—it's a total surprise!"

Do be ready to stop, drop, and roll from the flames of anger if your in-laws feel slighted. Only one relative has the honor of hearing first. Someone must hear it second and third, unless you carry out an ambitious conference call. If geography separates you, give your in-laws a call sooner rather than later. It's best not to wait until you see them in person—by then you could be holding a baby. If you can't catch them because, silly you, you called during their weekly salsa dancing class, leave a friendly and informative message:

> Hi! It's your daugher-in-law, Susan. Remember me? Well, finally your son and I had reproductive sex. Weirdly, it was after we had dinner two months ago when you were in town!

> Remember that? Yeah, I was so drunk. Anyhoo . . . now we're having a baby. Cra-zay! Guess we should get health insurance, soon! Byeeee!

After you hang up, discuss why your partner's voice is still on the machine since he hasn't lived with his parents in fifteen years. (What's up with that?)

Having a baby is a joyous occasion to be shared and celebrated. You only get nine months to bask in all the attention. After you deliver, the spotlight will shine on your drooling Winston Churchill look-alike poop machine. Did I say that?—I meant adorable baby.

### Judge Judy-in-Law

In-laws judge everything. They whisper about the dangers of your weight-lifting routine—"It's too disruptive for the baby." They wonder why you're still traveling for work (with that belly-button piercing no less). And they're apoplectic about the two cats living with you. Kill them! Give them back to the shelter! They're toxoplasmosistic monsters!

Of course, you never used to be their business. But once you started growing an heir to their throne and they placed the ultrasound photo in a gilded gold frame, you became their business.

How do you deal with the litany of in-law opinions?

- **Discover who your in-laws deify.** Use that person to thinly veil your "offensive activity" by stating that your doctor, Barbara Walters, or Vince Lombardi said that it's great for the baby. Now your in-law will respond with: "Oh, is that what they are doing now? Pregnant women are encouraged to go to rock concerts? Senator John McCain said music is good for the baby? Okay!"

- **Buy them a pregnancy book that's been printed in this century.** That way they can marvel at how much "times have changed." Now when you pass on the deli meats your in-laws purchased in your honor, you can refer them to page 200, while you eat folic acid–fortified cereal with pasteurized milk.
- **Keep the blinders on.** When your in-laws tell you "the truth" about permanent post-pregnancy body changes, pretend you're talking to Linda Blair from *The Exorcist*. Do you see your in-law's head spinning? Hear the gibberish? Every person's experience with pregnancy is unique. Your hips might return. You might have a lifetime with those Double D's! Your stretch marks may never disappear. You don't know, so stop worrying until you have to.

### Naming the Alien Growing Inside You

If only your in-laws suggested the names: Harry, George, or David. You could work with that. When they start throwing old family names at you: Agnes or Gertrude, Schlomo or Xaniophilides, there's cause to pause. Clearly, they're trying to get your child beaten up at preschool.

If *you* are the guilty party and you want to name your baby Zappa instead of Frank, remember this isn't a nom de plume. This is your kid's name *for life*. When in-laws don't like your selected name, they'll ask four questions every hour, on the hour:

1. "What does that mean?"
2. "How do you spell it?"
3. "We really like Tina. *Tina*. T-I-N-A."
4. "Do you know our family tradition of naming girls Tina?"

In response, you stand at a tall podium, with a laser pointer and a PowerPoint presentation, and explain to your in-laws how to spell your future child's name. You lecture about the cherished history of the name and why, above all, it's perfect. Horns blare. Drums roll. In summary, your child is destined for greatness. The writing is on the wall.

Exactly an hour later, your in-laws will ask: "How about Tina? That's a nice name." This is their not-so-subtle way of saying, "We'll be calling her Tina." Be strong, it's not that hard to spell Zappa. Your in-laws manage to spell their own crazy names.

The secret to naming a baby is not to tell anyone! If you must, you're bound to get a mouthful. Below is a chart with "the names heard around the in-law world" and the feelings they conjure:

**Baby Name Your In-Laws Pick**

| Name | What You Think | What Your In-Law Thinks |
|---|---|---|
| Jesus | "I hope they're thinking in Spanish." | "He'll be glorious." |
| Pajamas | "What the *hell*?" | "It's Pa' jamas. The first part is accented." |
| Winifred | "What about Katie? They make Katie charm necklaces." | "Our dead grandmother will be so pleased." |
| Anne | "That's nice." | "That's nice." |
| Damien | "Isn't that the devil's name?" | "It's a proper biblical name." |

**Baby Name You Pick**

| Name | What You Think | What Your In-Law Thinks |
|---|---|---|
| Boris | "It's a throwback name." | "Are we naming a pet?" |
| Arachna | "What a cool name." | "I knew my daughter-in-law was weird." |
| Esperanza | "It means hope." | "Apparently it means hope." |
| Joseph | "It's my father's name, his father's name, and his father's name." | "It's like *One Hundred Years of Solitude*. Everyone has the same name." |
| Rubin | "He'll be a ladykiller." | "A sandwich?!" |

Okay, so now you've selected a name. One that you think is perfect. Now watch it grow in the elaborate Game of Telephone your in-laws are playing. Here's a quick 12-hour snapshot of the in-law phone tree . . .

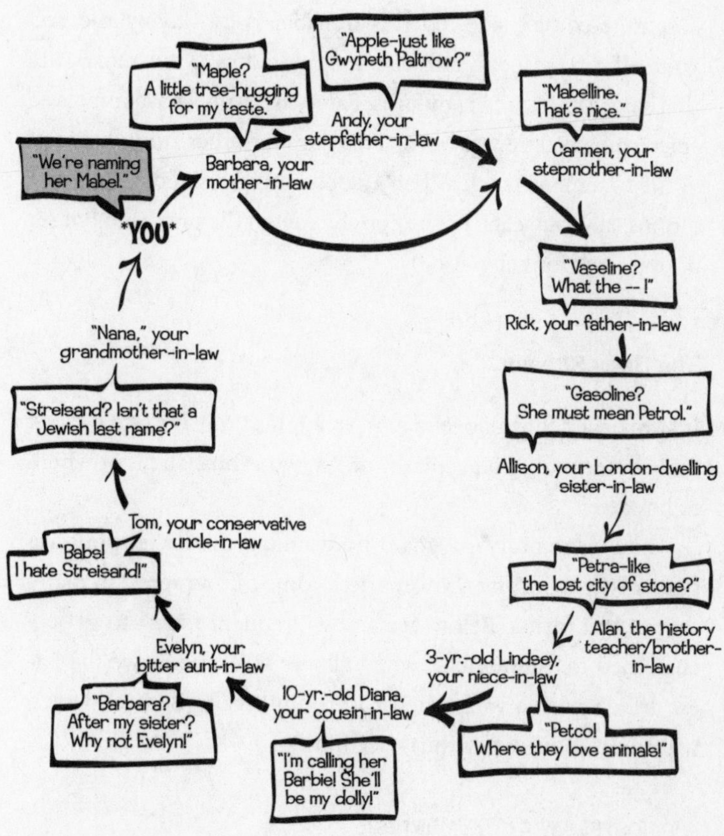


### Baby's New Castle

Slatted. Stylish. And white. The grandparent who plunks down his or her credit card to buy your baby's crib is the most revered grandparent. It is the honor of all honors. It's the gold standard of love. Aristotle once said: "He who buys the crib has bragging rights to family and friends, because they alone, above all others, provide shelter to a needy naked babe. He who is unable to provide the crib dies a slow, shameful death as a lowly provider of burp cloths."

If your in-laws and parents are in a race to buy your baby's first mini-condo, sidestep this hullabaloo by buying the crib yourself. Or, accept a crib as a hand-me-down. But make sure that said crib is up to standards. Safety measures have improved since your sweetie was born. This goes for other "found objects in the basement" such as baby gates, walkers, sleepwear, breast pumps, and car seats. Let's keep the eye on the prize and not set booby traps for baby.

## The Baby Shower

It's your wedding all over again. Only this time, it's two o'clock in the afternoon, you can't drink, and your husband is nowhere to be seen.

Like your puffy, pregnant body, in-law family tensions are bound to swell. Baby shower crises come gift-wrapped in many shapes and forms. Below are a few "frequent fliers" to get accustomed to. Remember, when all else fails, rise above the latest drama with a well-timed bathroom break. (Both of which will come about every thirty seconds.)

### THE HOSTESS WITH THE MOSTEST:

Oh, how your in-laws and your family will jockey to host your shower. It's enough to exhaust an already exhausted pregnant woman.

YOUR MOTHER: We wanted to host the baby shower, but with the cats . . . it just wouldn't work.

YOUR MOTHER-IN-LAW: Really? We had Fluffy put down so we could host the shower. That's how much we love Baby Addison.

Ask a friend to sponsor the party in a neutral location. That way there won't be an allegiance to a particular parent, in-law, or step-in-law. It's like the UN without flags.

THE SQUEAKY WHEEL:
Your soon-to-be-married sister-in-law loathes sharing attention. At your shower, she all but puts on her wedding dress and parades around the room.

YOUR SISTER-IN-LAW: Hello? Does anyone want to see *my* engagement ring? It's so pretty.

YOUR MOTHER-IN-LAW: You want to feel the baby kicking? Put your hand here!

YOUR SISTER-IN-LAW: Look how my diamond catches the light when the baby kicks it. I'm so happy I got a cushion cut.

Go ahead, be magnanimous. It's good practice for motherhood. Let her believe that not only is the event all about her ("Hey, have you guys seen Ted's sister's engagement ring? Isn't it GORGEOUS?"), it's a great opportunity to learn from your mistakes and make *her* baby shower the best thing since Johnson's & Johnson's No Tears Shampoo. Remember to give an extra big hug to her fiancé the next time you see him. *Does he know what he's getting himself into?*

HOUSE OF FLYING DAGGERS:
Look around the room. Do you spot those jealous eyes—in-laws still waiting to get pregnant after in vitro fertilization no. five? Don't let envy spoil the day. Keep your friends close, your in-law

enemies closer. Include these ladies in gift opening, game organizing, and photographing—your weary hands could use a break. If you're still choking from the stench of the green-eyed monster, hang a Turkish "evil eye" talisman in your home. It will protect you and your baby from the harmful thoughts of in-law relatives.

### FLEXING THE GOLD CARD:

What happens when all the women in your life congregate in a living room for four hours to share horrific birth stories, lasagna recipes, and opinions on the practicality of one another's baby gifts? They compete.

YOUR GRANDMOTHER: A silver Tiffany's rattle? What's the point of that?

YOUR GRANDMOTHER-IN-LAW: It's a keepsake.

YOUR GRANDMOTHER: Why not something useful—like diapers. What kind of idiot buys a rattle?

YOUR GRANDMOTHER-IN-LAW: I bought it.

YOUR GRANDMOTHER: Figures. Such a waste of money. I got her the Bugaboo baby jogger.

If you feel your baby shower is degenerating into a game of gift-giving one-upmanship, give yourself a gift: elevate your swollen feet, promise yourself a prenatal massage (it's amazing what a little self-bribery can accomplish), and enjoy the show. After all, baby doesn't know the difference between a Hermès onesie and a Kmart original. Thankfully you're only a week away from birth and meeting Ms. Feelgood Hormone Oxytocin. She's the stiff drink that you're looking for.

"My sister-in-law jump-started the economy the day she was pregnant and walked into Liz Lange, so I didn't have to. But she was a drug pusher with her hand-me-downs. I wasn't sure what to wear for my baby shower and she insisted on this pale blue dress that she wore to hers. Was I a doll? My ass is the size of a piano! Pale blue?! Finally, I had to tell her that our styles were too different. I kept a few T-shirts she loaned me, but had to return the rest. Sometimes it's a mixed blessing to have an in-law give you clothes! Be warned!"

NANCY, LONG ISLAND CITY

## Birth and Newborn

The miracle of life is painful, bloody, and terrifying. And for some reason, every one of your in-laws wants to document it on film and post it on YouTube.

### The Velvet Rope

Your in-laws line up, because Citysearch rated "The Delivery Room" a 9.8 out of 10. Your doctor checks IDs, while your doula and brother-in-law grind in the corner.

If your in-laws aren't invited into the delivery room, they'll feel snubbed. Your sister-in-law will never forgive you. Your uncle-in-law wants to wipe your sweaty brow—I mean you two are close, right? You might be a little hopped up on the epidural, but we're still talking about a scenario where your legs are up in the air with your hoo-hoo on display! They weren't invited the other times that happened! What's wrong with these people?

> "I didn't want to offend my father-in-law, but I just couldn't have him in the delivery room with me. I had no idea what to expect from birth, but he was determined to welcome his grandson into the world. Luckily for me I walked to the cafeteria alone with my husband to grab some water and gave birth right then and there. I was able to avoid my father-in-law, but everyone at the salad bar got a good show."
>
> BETSY, NEW YORK

Be firm about the rules. If you don't want anyone in the room, lock the door. If you want your in-laws to witness your successful water birth or hypnobirth to prove it was the best way to go, pack 'em in. Otherwise the more people in the room, the more likely you are to scream at them.

It's your prerogative to do as you please. Keep in mind that many of the same body parts involved in the conception are going to be there for everyone to see, only this time, a lot messier and without the scented candles. If they weren't in the room for the beginning, there's no reason they need to be there in the end. Besides, those copies of *Entertainment Weekly* in the waiting room aren't going to just read themselves.

Your in-laws will have an easier time adjusting to your rules if you tell them in advance and not while you're sucking on ice chips, shuffling the hospital halls in a paper gown. Here's a cheat sheet for what to say to your in-laws when they ask for an invitation:

**If you don't want your in-laws in the delivery room, say:**

1. "We're looking forward to being with you as a family after the birth. We wouldn't want you to travel twice!"
2. "It's a cesarean. I'll be in the boring ole OR—nothing to see!"

3. "There's no 'above the sheet' line, where you only see from my stomach on up. Just so you know."

**If you want your in-laws *and* your own parents in the delivery room, say:**

1. "I guess you all gave birth at some point. Come one; come all."
2. "Hey, this epidural is great. Are you my mom?"
3. "Look everyone—I shaved! And I'm crowning!"

**If you don't want *anyone* in the delivery room, say:**

1. "We'll see you guys at home!"
2. "I want to experience this with my doctor, nurse, and husband. You do not fit any of these categories."
3. "I'm so honored you want to be a part of my life. It would be great if you could feed the fish. Thanks for helping!"

## The Foreskin and You

Okay, you managed not to offend your Jewish and Asian in-laws by naming your baby after a living relative. Good job. But as you push and pant in labor, your in-laws will clasp your hand at the bedside and plead: "If you don't baptize, christen, perform a bris, or host a baby-naming ceremony for this child, we failed as parents."

It's just human nature—your in-laws want the best for their grandkid. And they believe their thousands of years of cultural tradition will ensure that. If you and yours haven't been clear how you plan to honor your baby's birth, in the first few incredible moments of your child's life, your in-laws will excitedly invite friends and family to the following:

- The Japanese naming ceremony, to be held in seven days, when your baby will be given a first and last name with no middle name.
- The Jewish *zeved habat* ceremony or the *berit milah* ceremony in eight days.
- The Hindu *namkaran* in 12 days, commemorated with a *havan* (sacred fire), and by writing your baby's name in the *janam patri* (Hindu astrological document).
- The Buddhist "fire-hair shaving" ceremony in one month and one day.
- The Islamic tradition, where the Call to Prayer is whispered into the newborn's right ear as the first sound it hears, symbolically bringing your baby into an awareness of Allah from the first moment of life.
- The Sikh ceremony at the *gurdwara*, where they will read a special Sikh prayer and drop *amrit* (holy water) on the baby's tongue, and choose the baby's name by opening the *Guru Granth Sahib* at random and deciding that the name begins with the first letter of first word of the *Hukamnama* on the left-hand side of the page.
- The Sierra Leone celebration, where as soon as your baby's umbilical cord falls off they will shave your baby's hair and invite your aunt-in-law to offer the baby chewed kola nut and pepper from her own mouth.

It's an incredible gift to raise your baby in a world of tradition and culture and have your little one showered with love from both families. But whatever you decide to do for your new family is your decision alone. Do not be bamboozled into cultural traditions with which you feel uncomfortable, or which are at odds with your and your sweetie's vision for how baby should be raised.

**Rule #1:** Remind your families that the best way to create a loving, respectful environment for their grandchild is to lay off the tug-of-war and lay on the c-o-m-p-r-o-m-i-s-e.

**Rule #2:** If you're an interfaith family, create a ceremony that reflects your values, beliefs, family, and the joy that is your baby. Blend traditions together with the help of an interfaith minister to honor parents, grandparents, siblings, and friends (i.e., godparents, spiritual mentors). Select special readings, prayers, blessings, and rituals. Remember all languages can be adapted for an intercultural assembly of in-laws.

**Rule #3:** When in doubt, refocus on the miracle at hand. You have a healthy, beautiful baby. When you feel like you're being guilted and pulled in a million different directions, focus on that little face. Gain the strength to be a mom and tell everyone what to do!

## The Parenting Lesson

It's week two of your newborn's life, and your mother-in-law is visiting for ten days. This is lovely if you two are close. I mean, what better way to spend time than with a woman who raised your sweetie, cooks like a champ, or can order in falafel with the best of them! This is a welcomed visit; your in-law will relieve some of the baby burden. Along with your newborn, you drool with delight.

However, if you and your in-law are not that close, it can be stressful. Not only is your body going haywire and acting in unpredictable ways, you'll be forced to hold conversations while sitting on the can. (Don't they understand a closed door means no talkie?) Who are these interlocutors in your life? They're not even helping!

Your in-law only seems interested in offering advice and analyzing the thread count of your sheets—barely half the time is the advice relevant to newborn care. The other half is about how best to rearrange your bedroom furniture or balance a checkbook. Last you checked you were a new mother, not a child. *Sigh.*

> "During my father-in-law's visit when my son was a newborn, he constantly corrected my grammar. He would line-edit my homemade notes—he's intolerant of split infinitives and incorrect pronouns. He would say nicely: 'It's between him and her not him and she, darling.' I know he can't help himself; he's an English professor. It just drove me crazy when I was already going out of my mind. I mean, I need help with the laundry and changing diapers, not my dangling modifiers!"
>
> PAMELA, MINNEAPOLIS

> "My mother-in-law always acted like she knew what was best. It didn't help that she was a Lamaze instructor for 20 years and the head of the La Leche league (something that strikes fear in most new mothers). Psychologically, it was hard to be reminded that my in-law was so learned in baby rearing. At first I was so insecure. Blame it on the hormones or my general overwhelmed state. Eventually, I began to feign confidence and say: 'Thank you for your advice, but I prefer to do it my way.' It was important for me to establish that role as caretaker, even if she was 90 percent right all the time."
>
> HEIDI, JACKSONVILLE

Whichever in-law is visiting, be it your mother-in-law, stepmother-in-law, or brother-in-law, you and the in-law will stare at each other in the living room *from morning until night.*

All the while, your baby alternates between sleeping and wailing, and most of the time your boobs are exposed. Sometimes your baby cries for more than an hour. You're about to lose your mind, when one of your many visiting in-laws yells:

All of the above statements make you feel as though you missed the memo of good mothering. It could be in that enormous pile of mail on the counter. I mean, Jimmy Hoffa could be buried in that mail pile. It *is* quite large.

Your in-law might actually have some useful information to impart on how to hold the baby or how to comfort the crying child. You're just annoyed by how they couch their advice. Also, you might be a little sensitive (you did cry at that emotive GE commercial this morning).

Let's be honest: *you* birthed this little person. So you don't know precisely how to deal with your baby's acne, yellowish eye discharge, cradle cap, and umbilical cord stump—so what! Sixteen-year-olds give birth in highway restrooms and do fine (well, sort of). You're way ahead of the curve! With a little reading, 3 AM reassurance from your doctor, and advice from your in-law (even if it pains you tremendously), you'll figure it out. Promise. By the way, most remedies involve water and a cottonball. It's pretty simple.

## Oh, Give Him Some Wine!

The last time your in-laws raised a kid was probably when Nixon was president. They can't help but give outdated baby advice.

Sure, they have learned a thing or two in their day. They know a lot about Rutherford B. Hayes, how to make a bed with hospital corners, and how to change a flat tire. However, they're not au courant about baby-caring techniques. They encourage you to pile more blankets and pillows into that "empty crib of yours." If you have in-laws who last raised kids in the 1970s, they will say:

- *"If you pick up the baby when he/she cries, you'll spoil him/her."* You know what? Spoil them! We *are* talking about babies and not teenagers. You can't shower enough love and attention on an infant. Babies aren't manipulative. They're not crying to taunt you (even if you think they are).
- *"They'll never learn to walk, if you keep carrying them."* Loving and smothering your baby will not prevent it from learning to walk. That's just crazy-speak.
- *"Don't nurse for too long, it's not good for the baby."* Breastfeeding is single-handedly the best thing you can do as a mother (that and not letting Michael Jackson come anywhere near your child). Breast milk makes for a stronger immune system, a more alert baby, and a healthy mom.
- *"Seriously, give him some wine!"* Wine works wonders when applied to the gums of a teething babe. But so does Orajel.

It's up to baby whether they like a full-bodied pinot noir or not. And I'm guessing—not.

- *"Every baby needs a large metal truck to play with."* Your in-laws played with toys that poked eyes out. They also used sleds that crippled. How charming! There's no need for little baby to play with Mister Rusty, the Tonka truck, with the plethora of stuffed-animal kitties and puppies in the world.
- *"Let baby crawl on the restaurant floor. It strengthens the immune system."* With that logic, why don't you let baby lick the bottom of your shoes? Or play in garbage bins—they're slimy, cool caves! Socializing and immersing baby into the world is enough of a jolt to the immune system. You don't need them to crawl around a roadside rest stop or suck on a car key to ward off influenza.

What should you say to your in-laws? "I appreciate your advice and insight; however, I'm more comfortable doing it this way." Or just lie: "Thank you, I'll have to try that." Another option is to strap the Baby Bjorn to your in-law and send them out into the glorious, outside world. Go! Flee! Be gone! Your in-law will receive so many compliments about their beautiful grandchild that they'll start thinking you know what you're doing after all.

### Hello Babysitters!

Your in-laws adore your child as much as you do. Now, with their babysitting generosity, you are able to grocery shop with free hands, sit calmly for a stylish haircut, and carry on adult conversations with adult friends without your nursing bra open and left nipple hanging out.

Of course, within the first ten minutes of your newfound freedom, you obsess over whether your child is acting sweet or demonic. Don't worry; your little one is the apple of your in-laws' eyes. Short of holding them at gunpoint, their grandkid can do no wrong. In fact, they would probably marvel that he can hold his head up at four months along with that pistol. He's a prodigy!

Keep in mind, though, that your in-laws' eagerness to run a day care center doesn't directly translate into their being the best option. In-law babysitters fall into two camps: they will either try to prove themselves worthy of child care (to the point of exhaustion) or they will crumble, from years of "growing soft."

> "I left my five-month-old son with my mother-in-law. She agreed to call me if he cried. When I got back, I found my house in lockdown mode. The windows were shut. The shades were drawn. The inside doors were closed. In the back room, my son was asleep. I mean, it looked fine, but my home felt a little like a prison. I can see why my husband is so disciplined now!"
>
> JESSICA, DAYTON

> "My mother-in-law offered to babysit and I jumped at the opportunity. She's a gentle woman and I trust her immensely. I was so excited to see a movie with my girlfriends, but ten minutes into the previews my mother-in-law called me. My baby was inconsolable. I rushed home to find my daughter smiling. It's going to take coaching, but she'll be up to babysitting speed eventually, and someday I'll finish the movie."
>
> BESS, FAIRFIELD

With guidance, you can mold your in-laws. Help them evolve into Grade-A babysitters. Really, you have no choice—they're free of cost, can be called at the last moment, and are around for years. Let's hope that your in-laws are eager Daniel Larussos to your Mr. Miyagi. Oh, how the tables have turned.

## The "Beyond" Years

You made it. You're confident—maybe even downright cocky. You've kept your two-year-old alive, which is the direct result of good parenting. And guess what's even better news? The relationship with your in-laws grows stronger when your baby is a toddler.

Toddlers are easier with in-laws than babies, because they express their needs. If they're hot, they're vocal. If they're thirsty, they tug on your sleeve. Your child is now his or her own little person. If they don't like something their grandmother-in-law is doing, they tell her.

> "My mother-in-law is an obsessive picture taker. I woke up at 7 AM the other morning and I could hear her in my daughter's room. She was asking her if she could take some photos. Is the camera in her bathrobe? I'm pretty sure my child will go blind from the flash bulbs, but she seems to like it. If she didn't, I know she'd say something. I had to laugh, when my daughter started to ham it up. Clearly, she doesn't think my mother-in-law is as annoying as I do."
>
> LAURA, SPOKANE

You see the love between your child and your in-law, and it sweetens you. Suddenly any annoying habit, gesture, or question from your in-law doesn't bear the same weight it once did. However, along with the burgeoning upside to your babysitting and loving in-laws and your now-speaking and independent toddler, you inherit a few new challenges:

- When your in-law visits, you must dress your child in whatever your in-law has purchased. Get used to it: your child is a show pony. This translates into five costume changes in a 24-hour period of homemade neon painted onesies that read "Grandma's Lil' Stinker."
- You must travel. A lot. Everybody wants to see your adorable darling! Older in-law relatives may have difficulty reaching you, so you must go to them. We're talking at least five hours in the car during holiday seasons. A two-year-old buckled into the backseat of a car in holiday traffic with a talking Nemo fish! Does it get any better?
- You must endure the "when are you having another child?" question. Your in-laws inquire every single moment that you're together. You answer: "I don't know" when you take out the trash, when you add steaks to the BBQ grill, and when you check your e-mail. Take this as a compliment. You did good, kid. Your in-laws just want a sequel.

In conclusion, a baby can bring you and your in-laws closer. When your in-laws shower love and devotion on your child they are, in turn, loving you, too.

At this point in your relationship, you can't help but feel connected to your mother-in-law and father-in-law. You fully appreciate the sacrifices they made as parents. You're now more likely to send "Just Saying Hi" cards to your in-laws. It's easy; your child scribbles three lines with crayons on construction paper and voilà, you pop it in the mail. Your in-laws love it! Earn even more points if you send something on Mother-in-Law Day, which is the fourth Sunday in October (established in 1981).

As for overbearing in-law parental advice, appreciate the baby-rearing gems. Maybe they offhandedly taught you something about clearing diaper rash or they clipped a helpful newspaper article about tips for baby's bath time. Maybe by accident they turned on the vacuum cleaner when your baby was crying and it serendipitously stopped the tears.

Whatever happens, you're in it together. You understand why your mother-in-law and father-in-law have the memory of an elephant with a Ph.D. Any time your little child yawns, smiles, or poops, your in-laws declare that your husband did the exact same thing *in the exact same way.*

How can they really remember that? You barely remember what you did this morning, let alone what happened twenty years ago. The truth is your in-laws can't.

They're just reliving their wonderful years as parents, aunts, and uncles to your sweetie. They're remembering a time when they were needed and loved. Is it so bad to smile along with them and say you see the same thing?

You'll be in the same boat in thirty years' time, when your little one will fall in love with someone other than you. *Sigh.*

# author's note

If you have ever thought that you did something to upset your in-laws, just remember you didn't write a book about them. People ask me: "Do your in-laws know about this book? How do they feel about it?" I reply: "They're really proud of me."

Of course, my in-laws were the inspiration for this book. The day I fell in love with my husband, I inherited brand-new family members. It was shocking suddenly to be thrust into the middle of a family's idiosyncrasies, like their use of the Socratic method at Passover seders: "Did Moses lead the Israelites across the Red Sea in 1200 BC! Or 1150 BC! Tell me!"

Hundreds of dinners, holidays, and vacations later, I'm still kicking and my in-laws are some of my best friends. Since this is a public forum, I feel compelled to finally set some things straight. Regrettably, I have done the following to my in-laws:

- Skied past my fallen father-in-law, leaving him in a snowbank
- Had a naked picture of myself accidentally shown to my mother- and father-in-law (damn iPhoto!)
- Sent incorrect wedding invitations to in-laws' immediate family
- Returned in-laws' car with front bumper and license plate missing
- Discovered in-laws' computer password is my name, but misspelled

So, my in-laws are all over this book. But they are far from being all of this book. The chapters are filled with personal experiences as well those researched and imagined.

Ladies, let this book be a start of great things for you and yours. Create strong allies and partners with your in-laws, and they will be a source of love and support in your life. Like they are in mine.

# acknowledgments

If not for the following people, the blinding work of brilliance you hold in your hands would not have been possible:

*Stephanie Kip Rostan:* for finding a nurturing home for my imagination. I'm forever lucky for your guidance, wit, and bottomless reservoir of sarcasm.

*Sarah Knight,* Ms. Editor Extraordinaire: a first-time author can't ask for a better partner in crime. Your humor, track changes from Judd Harris, and late nights (okay, many late nights) are forever appreciated.

*Muffy & Nina:* You ladies. You guys. Are hilarious. I only hope I'm half the friend to you as you are to me. Notes by tomorrow? Thanks.

*Fran, Stefanie, Greg, Manoush, Josh, Cristina, Ada, Ellen, Yi-Wyn, and Nicole:* You endured my endless yammering. You read. You are gold.

*Mom, Dad, Jamie:* You taught me to notice the humor in everyday life. Mom, thanks for telling me to "go outside and get some fresh air." You're right. I should.

*David, Dr. Inexhaustible/husband:* Thank you for rubbing my shoulders, reading my pages, and hugging me. Twenty-two gazillion times a day. And that was before lunchtime.

# about the author

Dina Koutas Poch is a writer and filmmaker. She lives in New York City with her husband and two cats. Her in-laws live in Connecticut.

Her enthusiasms include running, playing tennis, yoga, and skiing. And, when not athletically engaged, watching or writing films, she tinkers around the kitchen, learning how to cook *authentic* Greek food.

She holds a B.A. from Brown University and a M.F.A. from Columbia University. She's been a film archivist for Getty Images and a fund-raising writer for the president of Brown University. This is her first book.